2,715
One-Line
Quotations
for Speakers,
Writers &
Raconteurs

2,715
One-Line
Quotations
for Speakers,
Writers &
Raconteurs

Edward F. Murphy

A HERBERT MICHELMAN BOOK
CROWN PUBLISHERS, INC.   NEW YORK

Inquiries should be addressed to Crown Publishers, Inc., One Park Avenue, New York, New York 10016

Printed in the United States of America

Published simultaneously in Canada by General Publishing Company Limited

Library of Congress Cataloging in Publication Data

Murphy, Edward F 1921–
2,715 one-line quotations for speakers, writers & raconteurs.

  "A Herbert Michelman book."
  I. Quotations, English. I. Title.
PN6081.M88 1981   082   80-24320
ISBN: 0-517-54281 1

10 9 8 7 6 5 4 3 2

FOR TERRY

and the delicious fruit of our collaboration,
Paula, Maria, and Jeanne

ACKNOWLEDGMENTS

With warmest thanks to my wife, Theresa, who typed the entire manuscript and was supportive in many ways.

A word of appreciation, too, to the late Herbert Michelman who suggested this collection.

2,715 One-Line Quotations for Speakers, Writers & Raconteurs

ABILITY

Anything you're good at contributes to happiness.

BERTRAND RUSSELL

Men take only their needs into consideration—never their abilities.

NAPOLEON BONAPARTE

Ability: The art of getting credit for all the home runs that somebody else hits.

CASEY STENGEL

Skill and confidence are an unconquered army.   GEORGE HERBERT

A good rooster crows in any hen house.

NORTH CAROLINA FOLK SAYING

The king is the man who can.   THOMAS CARLYLE

I get quiet joy from the observation of anyone who does his job well.

WILLIAM C. FEATHER

ACCEPTANCE

I not only bow to the inevitable; I am fortified by it.

THORNTON WILDER

Make the best use of what is in your power, and take the rest as it happens.

EPICTETUS

Every wrong seems possible today, and is accepted. I don't accept it.

PABLO CASALS

My old father used to have a saying: If you make a bad bargain, hug it all the tighter.

ABRAHAM LINCOLN

Everything in life that we really accept undergoes a change.

KATHERINE MANSFIELD

ACHIEVEMENT

It is not enough to aim, you must hit.   ITALIAN PROVERB

To achieve great things we must live as if we were never going to die.

VAUVENARGUES

I

Back of every achievement is a proud wife and a surprised mother-in-law.   BROOKS HAYS

Now that it's all over, what did you really do yesterday that's worth mentioning?   COLEMAN COX

The world recognizes nothing short of performance, because performance is what it needs, and promises are of no use to it.

PHILIP G. HAMERTON

ACTION

One's action ought to come out of an achieved stillness: not to be a mere rushing on.   D. H. LAWRENCE

Action springs not from thought, but from a readiness for responsibility.   DIETRICH BONHOEFFER

Thunder is good, thunder is impressive; but it is the lightning that does the work.   MARK TWAIN

Action is eloquence.   SHAKESPEARE

Be content to act, and leave the talking to others.

BALTASAR GRACIAN

Things don't turn up in this world until somebody turns them up.

JAMES A. GARFIELD

I begin to think that a calm is not desirable in any situation in life. Man was made for action and for bustle, too, I believe.

ABIGAIL ADAMS

ACTORS AND ACTING

An actor's popularity is fleeting. His success has the life expectancy of a small boy who is about to look into a gas tank with a lighted match.   FRED ALLEN

Acting: An art which consists of keeping the audience from coughing.   SIR RALPH RICHARDSON

The only thing you owe the public is a good performance.

HUMPHREY BOGART

I would take a bad script and a good director any day against a good script and a bad director. BETTE DAVIS

Acting is the most immediate art of all. The audience is either caught up entirely or not; it's now or nothing. MICHAEL REDGRAVE

I can't for the life of me see what nudity has to do with good acting. But perhaps if I were younger I would feel differently

JULIE HARRIS

ADMIRATION

We always like those who admire us, but we do not always like those whom we admire. LA ROCHEFOUCAULD

We always admire the other fellow more after we have tried to do his job. WILLIAM C. FEATHER

We need to be taught to admire, to surrender ourselves to admiration. WILLIAM HALE WHITE

I never knew a man so mean that I was not willing he should admire me. E. W. HOWE

Admiration and familiarity are strangers. GEORGE SAND

It is almost impossible to find those who admire us entirely lacking in taste. J. PETIT-SENN

ADOLESCENCE

You don't have to suffer to be a poet. Adolescence is enough suffering for anyone. JOHN CIARDI

Why can't life's problems hit us when we're seventeen and know everything? A. C. JOLLY

From the age of twelve the adolescent feels the call of the flesh, but he is allowed no means of responding before, say, the age of eighteen. HENRI DE MONTHERLANT

There's nothing wrong with teenagers that reasoning with them won't aggravate. ANONYMOUS

In a world as empirical as ours, a youngster who does not know what he is good *at* will not be sure what he is good *for*.

EDGAR Z. FRIEDENBERG

In no order of things is adolescence the time of the simple life.

JANET ERSKINE STUART

ADULTERY

Adultery: Democracy applied to love.   H. L. MENCKEN

There's nothing in the world like the devotion of a married woman. It's a thing no married man knows anything about.

OSCAR WILDE

One man's folly is another man's wife.   HELEN ROWLAND

When a man says, "Get out of my home! What do you want my wife for?"—there is no need for an answer.   CERVANTES

No man worth having is true to his wife, or can be true to his wife, or ever was, or ever will be.   SIR JOHN VANBRUGH

Adultery introduces spirit into what otherwise might have been the dead letter of marriage.   MARCEL PROUST

He and I had an office so tiny that an inch smaller and it would have been adultery.   DOROTHY PARKER

ADVENTURE

Adventures are to the adventurous.   BENJAMIN DISRAELI

It's when you're safe at home that you wish you were having an adventure. When you're having an adventure you wish you were safe at home.   THORNTON WILDER

Without adventure civilisation is in full decay.

ALFRED NORTH WHITEHEAD

The most beautiful adventures are not those we go to seek.

ROBERT LOUIS STEVENSON

It is only in adventure that some people succeed in knowing themselves—in finding themselves.   ANDRÉ GIDE

But almost any place is Baghdad if you don't know what will happen in it.   EDNA FERBER

My favorite thing is to go where I've never been.   DIANE ARBUS

ADVERTISING

As a whole, advertising is committed to the ways of business, and as the ways of business are seldom straight and narrow, advertising perforce must follow a dubious path.   J. THORNE SMITH

Living in an age of advertisement, we are perpetually disillusioned.   J. B. PRIESTLEY

Advertising: Something which makes one think he's longed all his life for a thing he's never even heard of before.   ANONYMOUS

Advertising nourishes the consuming power of men. . . . It spurs individual exertion and greater production. SIR WINSTON CHURCHILL

The deeper problems connected with advertising come less from the unscrupulousness of our "deceivers" than from our pleasure in being deceived, less from the desire to seduce than from the desire to be seduced.   DANIEL J. BOORSTIN

ADVICE

I realize that advice is worth what it costs—that is, nothing.
DOUGLAS MAC ARTHUR

Less advice and more hands.   GERMAN PROVERB

As to advice, be wary: If honest, it is also criticism. DAVID GRAYSON

All of us, at certain moments of our lives, need to take advice and receive help from other people.   ALEXIS CARREL

It is only too easy to make suggestions and later try to escape the consequences of what we say.   JAWAHARLAL NEHRU

It is not good to give one's advice unasked.   JANET ERSKINE STUART

No one wants advice—only corroboration.   JOHN STEINBECK

Sometimes I give myself admirable advice, but I am incapable of taking it.   LADY MARY WORTLEY MONTAGU

It takes nearly as much ability to know how to profit by good advice as to know how to act for oneself.   LA ROCHEFOUCAULD

I never had a man come to me for advice yet, but what I soon discovered that he thought more of his own opinion than he did of mine.   JOSH BILLINGS

AGE

I'd rather have two girls at seventeen than one at thirty-four.
                                                    FRED ALLEN

The Grecian ladies counted their age from their marriage, not their birth.   HOMER

I don't believe one grows older. I think that what happens early on in life is that at a certain age one stands still and stagnates.
                                                    T. S. ELIOT

You've heard of the three ages of man—youth, age, and "you're looking wonderful."   FRANCIS CARDINAL SPELLMAN

Everyone is the age he has decided on, and I have decided to remain thirty years old.   PABLO PICASSO

How old would you be if you didn't know how old you were?
                                                    SATCHEL PAGE

There must be a day or two in a man's life when he is the precise age for something important.   FRANKLIN P. ADAMS

We are always the same age inside.   GERTRUDE STEIN

Nothing ages a man like living always with the same woman.
                                                    NORMAN DOUGLAS

I wonder if one of the penalties of growing older is that you become more and more conscious that nothing in life is very permanent.   ELEANOR ROOSEVELT

The older you get, the faster you ran when you were a kid.
                                                    STEVE OWEN

We grow old as soon as we cease to love and trust.
                                                    MADAME DE CHOISEUL

Somewhere in *The Poet and the Donkey,* Andy speaks for me when he says, "Do not deprive me of my age. I have earned it." MAY SARTON

I am old enough to see how little I have done in so much time, and how much I have to do in so little.   SHEILA KAYE-SMITH

AGE, MIDDLE

All this talk about puberty being so hard on kids. Puberty isn't in it with middle age, not by a damned sight.   JOHN DOS PASSOS

Middle age is when you're not inclined to exercise anything but caution.   ARTHUR MURRAY

Middle age is having a choice between two temptations and choosing the one that'll get you home earlier.   DAN BENNETT

Hostility to youth is the worst vice of the middle-aged.

J. A. SPENDER

An energetic middle life is, I think, the only safe precursor of a vitally happy old age.   VIDA D. SCUDDER

Of middle age the best that can be said is that a middle-aged person has likely learned how to have a little fun in spite of his troubles.   DON MARQUIS

In middle age we are apt to reach the horrifying conclusion that all sorrow, all pain, all passionate regret and loss and bitter disillusionment are self-made.   KATHLEEN NORRIS

Middle age is when you have met so many people that every new person you meet reminds you of someone else and usually is.

OGDEN NASH

From forty to fifty a man must move upward, or the natural falling off in the vigor of life will carry him rapidly downward.

OLIVER WENDELL HOLMES, JR.

Middle age: The time when you'll do anything to feel better, except give up what is hurting you.   ROBERT QUILLEN

AGE, OLD

Mostly it is the elderly who preserve a human link with the past and nourish an entire generation curious to know its full cultural heritage.   HEDRICK SMITH

People who don't cherish their elderly have forgotten whence they came and whither they go.   RAMSEY CLARK

It is quite wrong to think of old age as a downward slope. One climbs higher and higher with the advancing years, with surprising strides.   GEORGE SAND

Most people say that as you get old, you have to give up things. I think you get old because you give up things.

SEN. THEODORE F. GREEN,
at eighty-seven

When one finds company in himself and his pursuits, he cannot feel old, no matter what his years may be.   A. BRONSON ALCOTT

A man is not old as long as he is seeking something. JEAN ROSTAND

Whatever poet, orator, or sage may say of it, old age is still old age.
HENRY WADSWORTH LONGFELLOW

A man is not old until regrets take the place of dreams.

JOHN BARRYMORE

I begin to realize that I am growing old: The taxi driver calls me "Pop" instead of "Buddy."   ALEXANDER WOOLLCOTT

An elderly lady who was asked by a child if she were young or old said: "My dear, I have been young a very long time." ANONYMOUS

I fear vastly more a futile, incompetent old age than I do any form of death.   WILLIAM ALLEN WHITE

So long as you can keep on finding new places to go, new fields to look into, you don't get old very fast.   REX BEACH

We grow neither better nor worse as we get old, but more like ourselves.   MAY LAMBERTON BECKER

One cannot help being old, but one can resist being aged.

LORD SAMUEL

The chief thing about being no longer young is that . . . one is no longer young.   HAROLD NICHOLSON

I won't be old till my feet hurt, and they only hurt when I don't let 'em dance enough, so I'll keep right on dancing.

BILL ("BOJANGLES") ROBINSON

Never lose sight of the fact that old age needs so little but needs that little so much.   MARGARET WILLOUR

I am getting old and the sign of old age is that I begin to philosophize and ponder over problems which should not be my concern at all.   JAWAHARLAL NEHRU

ALONE

There are people whose society I find delicious; but when I sit alone and think of them, I shudder.   LOGAN PEARSALL SMITH

Every man who is truly a man must learn to be alone in the midst of all the others, and if need be against all the others.

ROMAIN ROLLAND

God created man, and, finding him not sufficiently alive, gave him a female companion to make him feel his solitude more keenly.

PAUL VALÉRY

Man is a gregarious animal, and much more so in his mind than in his body. He may like to go alone for a walk, but he hates to stand alone in his opinions.   GEORGE SANTAYANA

If I can by any means get myself to consider myself alone without reference to others, discontent will vanish.   WILLIAM HALE WHITE

Inside myself is a place where I live all alone, and that's where you renew your springs that never dry up.   PEARL BUCK

When it comes to the important things one is always alone.

MAY SARTON

AMBITION

I . . . had ambition not only to go farther than any man had ever been before, but as far as it was possible for a man to go.

CAPT. JAMES COOK

I have found some of the best reasons I ever had for remaining at the bottom simply by looking at the men at the top.

FRANK MOORE COLBY

But the moment you turn a corner you see another straight stretch ahead and there comes some further challenge to your ambition.

OLIVER WENDELL HOLMES, JR.

There is no eel so small but it hopes to become a whale.

GERMAN PROVERB

Ambition is the grand enemy of all peace.   JOHN COWPER POWYS

It is most important in this world to be pushing, but it is fatal to seem so.   BENJAMIN JOWETT

"One day," he says, "I too will be so rich that I shall have my photo on the bands of cigars I offer to my friends. That is my ambition."   JEAN RHYS

AMERICA

Intellectually I know that America is no better than any other country; emotionally I know she is better than every other country.
                                                    SINCLAIR LEWIS

Let America realize that self-scrutiny is not treason. Self-examination is not disloyalty.   RICHARD CARDINAL CUSHING

Whatever America hopes to bring to pass in the world must first come to pass in the heart of America.   DWIGHT D. EISENHOWER

If you have the habit, as I have, of reading what visitors to America think about our society, you have already discovered that in the last century they were likely to find our women a great deal better company than our men.   RUSSELL LYNES

We cannot reform the world. . . . Uncle Sugar is as dangerous a role for us to play as Uncle Shylock.   JOHN F. KENNEDY

I love the United States, but I see here everything is measured by success, by how much money it makes, not the satisfaction to the individual.   MARIA SCHELL

America has not always been kind to its artists and scholars. Somehow the scientists always seem to get the penthouse while the arts and humanities get the basement.   LYNDON B. JOHNSON

The problem is that Americans would like to be independent of the rest of the world. . . . Except the world ain't that way. Trying to be independent of the rest of the world is to commit suicide.
                                                    ANDREW YOUNG

America is so vast that almost everything said about it is likely to be true, and the opposite is probably equally true. JAMES T. FARRELL

An asylum for the sane would be empty in America.
                                          GEORGE BERNARD SHAW

If America ever passes out as a great nation, we ought to put on our tombstone: America died from a delusion she had Moral Leadership.   WILL ROGERS

We have plenty of Confidence in this country, but we are a little
short of good men to place our Confidence in.   WILL ROGERS

Perhaps this is our strange and haunting paradox here in America—that we are fixed and certain only when we are in movement.

THOMAS WOLFE

America is a nation with many flaws, but hopes so vast that only
the cowardly would refuse to acknowledge them. JAMES MICHENER

The thing that impresses me most about America is the way parents obey their children.   DUKE OF WINDSOR

Nothing would do more for our national health than a feeling that
we are engaged in enterprises touched with some kind of nobility
or grandeur.   RICHARD GOODWIN

All America has to do to get in bad all over the world is just to
start out on what we think is a Good Samaritan mission.

WILL ROGERS

Ours seems to be the only nation on earth that asks its teenagers
what to do about world affairs, and tells its golden-agers to go out
and play.   JULIAN GEROW

Here [in America] we write well when we expose frauds and hypo-
crites. We are great at counting warts and blemishes and weighing
feet of clay. In expressing love, we belong among the undeveloped
countries.   SAUL BELLOW

AMERICANS

Americans are damn good fighters when the muddling stage is over
and the fight begins.   HERVEY ALLEN

There is nothing the matter with Americans except their ideals;
the real American is all right; it is the ideal American who is all
wrong.   G. K. CHESTERTON

Americans like fat books and thin women.   RUSSELL BAKER

I like Americans. They always make an effort when they meet you.
They want to be liked and to like you; it is always easy to be with
them.   MARIA SCHELL

The overwhelming majority of Americans are possessed of two
great qualities—a sense of humor and a sense of proportion.

FRANKLIN D. ROOSEVELT

I am a firm believer in the people; and if given the truth, they can be depended upon to meet any national crisis.

DOUGLAS MAC ARTHUR

Only Americans can hurt America.   DWIGHT D. EISENHOWER

There is a sense in which every American, black or white, is affected by racism. You cannot grow up in the United States of America in the twentieth century and not be tainted by it.

ANDREW YOUNG

We dare not forget that we are the heirs of that first revolution.

JOHN F. KENNEDY

If Americans could only believe in America.

RAYMOND CLAPPER

[Americans] expect to eat and stay thin, to be constantly on the move and ever more neighborly.   DANIEL J. BOORSTIN

The general belief still is that Americans are not destined to renounce, but to enjoy.   HERBERT CROLY

Americans think of themselves collectively as a huge rescue squad on twenty-four-hour call to any spot on the globe where dispute and conflict may erupt.   ELDRIDGE CLEAVER

An American woman who respects herself must buy something every day of her life.   HENRY JAMES

The American never imitates the Englishman in simply taking for granted his own patriotism and his own superiority.

G. K. CHESTERTON

American: One who will cheerfully respond to every appeal except to move back in a bus.   ANONYMOUS

The word which gives the key to the national vice is waste.

HENRY MILLER

One characteristic of Americans is that they have no tolerance at all of anybody putting up with anything. We believe that whatever is going wrong ought to be fixed.   MARGARET MEAD

The more money an American accumulates, the less interesting he becomes.   GORE VIDAL

ANGER

There is something about a roused woman . . . especially if she add to all her other strong passions the fierce impulses of recklessness and despair . . . which few men like to provoke. CHARLES DICKENS

Hate is a kind of "passive suffering," but indignation is a kind of joy. WILLIAM B. YEATS

People who fly into a rage always make a bad landing.

WILL ROGERS

There is nothing more galling to angry people than the coolness of those on whom they wish to vent their spleen. ALEXANDRE DUMAS

If we are deprived of our just due, we naturally experience emotions of anger. DR. SMILEY BLANTON

Powerless rage can work miracles. STANISLAW J. LEC

When I am right, I get angry. Churchill gets angry when he is wrong. So we were often angry at each other. CHARLES DE GAULLE

ANIMALS

It often happens that a man is more humanely related to a cat or dog than to any human being. HENRY DAVID THOREAU

Some people lose all respect for the lion unless he devours them instantly. There is no pleasing some people. WILL CUPPY

We have enslaved the rest of the animal creation, and have treated our distant cousins in fur and feathers so badly that beyond doubt, if they were able to formulate a religion, they would depict the Devil in human form. WILLIAM R. INGE

The Puritans objected to bearbaiting not because it gave pain to the bear but because it gave pleasure to the spectators.

THOMAS MACAULAY

There is certainly something very touching about lambs, until they find their way into holy pictures and become unpleasant.

THOMAS MERTON

ANSWER

People of many kinds ask questions, but few and rare people listen to answers. Why?   JANET ERSKINE STUART

It is a good answer that knows when to stop.   ITALIAN PROVERB

She has the answer to everything and the solution to nothing.

OSCAR LEVANT

ANXIETY

It is well to remind ourselves that anxiety signifies a conflict, and so long as a conflict is going on, a constructive solution is possible.

ROLLO MAY

Anxiety and distress, interrupted occasionally by pleasure, is the normal course of man's existence.   JOSEPH WOOD KRUTCH

We find our energies are actually cramped when we are overanxious to succeed.   MONTAIGNE

No good work is ever done while the heart is hot and anxious and fretted.   OLIVE SCHREINER

One cannot remove anxiety by arguing it away.   PAUL TILLICH

APPEARANCE

It must be great to be rich and let the other fellow keep up appearances.   KIN HUBBARD

I am sure that nothing has such a decisive influence upon a man's course as his personal appearance, and not so much his appearance as his belief in its attractiveness or unattractiveness.   LEO TOLSTOY

I think it is an obligation of every woman to look as nice as she can no matter what her age.   ELEANOR ROOSEVELT

Things do not pass for what they are, but for what they seem. Most things are judged by their jackets.   BALTASAR GRACIAN

The tragedy of our time is that we are so eye-centered, so appearance-besotted.   JESSAMYN WEST

It is only the shallow people who do not judge by appearances.

OSCAR WILDE

APPRECIATION

A little appreciation seems to me even more insidious than a little learning. It taints everything it touches and it touches everything, just the veneer of appreciation.   ANNE MORROW LINDBERGH

I now perceive one immense omission in my *Psychology*—the deepest principle of human nature is the *craving to be appreciated.*

WILLIAM JAMES

The question is not what a man can scorn, or disparage, or find fault with, but what he can love and value and appreciate.

JOHN RUSKIN

> A poor life this if, full of care,
> We have no time to stand and stare.

WILLIAM HENRY DAVIES

I expect that all of us get pretty much what we deserve of appreciation.

A. C. BENSON

ARGUMENT

The moment you grab someone by the lapels, you're lost.

BURT REYNOLDS

The man who sees both sides of a question is a man who sees absolutely nothing at all.   OSCAR WILDE

Discussion is an exchange of knowledge; argument an exchange of ignorance.   ROBERT QUILLEN

The greatest danger in any argument is that real issues are often clouded by superficial ones, that momentary passions may obscure permanent realities.   MARY ELLEN CHASE

The best argument is that which seems merely an explanation.

DALE CARNEGIE

More than once I have heard good men come out second best to demagogues in argument because they have depended on their righteous indignation and neglected their homework.

NORMAN THOMAS

Every argument between two people is likely to sink or rise to the level of a dogfight.   A. A. MILNE

ART

Art is meant to disturb.   GEORGES BRAQUE

There is nothing we can do to a work of art by either ignoring it or glaring at it, but there is a great deal it would like to do for us if we would give it half a chance.   RUSSELL LYNES

There is no surer method of evading the world than by following Art, and no surer method of linking oneself to it than by Art.

GOETHE

Art is nothing less than a way of making joys perpetual.

REBECCA WEST

Art is the difference between seeing and just identifying.

JEAN MARY MORMAN

It has been said that art is a tryst, for in the joy of it maker and beholder meet.   KOJIRO TOMITA

Surely nothing has to listen to so many stupid remarks as a painting in a museum.   EDMOND AND JULES DE GONCOURT

As far as I am concerned, a painting speaks for itself. What is the use of giving explanations, when all is said and done? A painter has only one language.   PABLO PICASSO

Art is either a plagiarist or a revolutionist.   PAUL GAUGUIN

ARTIST

The true painter strives to paint what can only be seen through his world.   ANDRÉ MALRAUX

Scratch an artist and you surprise a child.   JAMES G. HUNEKER

A subject that is beautiful in itself gives no suggestion to the artist. It lacks imperfection.   OSCAR WILDE

The artist's morality lies in the force and truth of his description.

JULES BARBEY D'AUREVILLY

An artist's career always begins tomorrow.

JAMES MC NEILL WHISTLER

In artistic work one needs nothing so much as conscience: It is the sole standard.   RAINER MARIA RILKE

Every time an artist dies, part of the vision of mankind passes with him.   FRANKLIN D. ROOSEVELT

ATTITUDE

No life is so hard that you can't make it easier by the way you take it.   ELLEN GLASGOW

It all depends on how we look at things, and not on how they are in themselves.   CARL G. JUNG

A stiff attitude is one of the phenomena of rigor mortis.

HENRY S. HASKINS

I am still determined to be cheerful and happy in whatever situation I may be, for I have also learned from experience that the greater part of our happiness or misery depends on our dispositions and not on our circumstances.   MARTHA WASHINGTON

We awaken in others the same attitude of mind we hold toward them.   ELBERT HUBBARD

Our attitudes toward the other sex correspond to our general approach toward life—toward any problem with which life confronts us.   DR. RUDOLF DREIKURS

AUTOMOBILE

The automobile is technologically more sophisticated than the bundling board, but the human motives in their uses are sometimes the same.   CHARLES M. ALLEN

I've found that an overlooked psychological factor contributing to auto accidents is the driver's dislike for his car.

DR. SHELDON ZIGELBAUM

Another way to solve the traffic problems of this country is to pass a law that only paid-for cars be allowed to use the highways.

WILL ROGERS

If you think nobody cares if you're alive, try missing a couple of car payments.   EARL WILSON

I drove back from Springfield with a reckless exultation at the fast, steady driving—powerful engine—along the road, my head up, singing all the way.   ANNE MORROW LINDBERGH

What a lucky thing the wheel was invented before the automobile; otherwise can you imagine the awful screeching?

SAMUEL HOFFENSTEIN

The greater part of my official time is spent on investigating collisions between propelled vehicles, each on its own side of the road, each sounding its horn, and each stationary.

AN ENGLISH LORD CHIEF JUSTICE

BACHELOR

Every man has it in his power to make one woman happy by remaining a bachelor.   DAISY F. AYRES

A bachelor is a man who can take a nap on top of a bedspread.

MARCELENE COX

A man without a wife is like a man in winter without a fur hat.

RUSSIAN PROVERB

Clear thoughts expressed in unclear language is the style of a confirmed bachelor. He never has to explain anything to a wife.

LIN YUTANG

Whoever is free from wrangling is a bachelor.   SAINT JEROME

To remain a woman's ideal, a man must die a bachelor.

ANONYMOUS

BASEBALL

I don't like them fellas who drive in two runs and let in three.

CASEY STENGEL

All I can tell 'em is I pick a good one and sock it. I get back to the dugout and they ask me what it was I hit and I tell 'em I don't know except it looked good.   BABE RUTH

Say this much for big league baseball—it is beyond any question the greatest conversation piece ever invented in America.

BRUCE CATTON

A baseball game is twice as much fun if you're seeing it on the company's time.   WILLIAM C. FEATHER

You can't be afraid to make mistakes. You've got to play the game aggressively.   LOU PINIELLA

There is no logical reason why girls shouldn't play baseball. It's not that tough.   HANK AARON

It's a business, cold and impersonal, and you have to adjust to that.

MIKE FLANAGAN

Hitting is so much mental, so much confidence. The technical part, the mechanical part, is overrated.   DAVE KINGMAN

It ain't nothin' till I call it.   BILL KLEM

A baseball park is the one place where a man's wife doesn't mind his getting excited over somebody else's curves.   BRENDAN FRANCIS

It seems the baseball player of today will not be satisfied until he plays two weeks in the big league and is able to retire at twenty-two.   JOE GARAGIOLA

The idea in this game isn't to win popularity polls or to be a good guy to everyone. The name of the game is *win*.   BILLY MARTIN

People always told me that my natural ability and good eyesight were the reasons for my success as a hitter. They never talk about the practice, practice, practice!   TED WILLIAMS

Sometimes the best deals are the ones you don't make. BILL VEECK

More than any other American sport, baseball creates the magnetic, addictive illusion that it can almost be understood.

THOMAS BOSWELL

The greater the pressure, the more I like it.   NOLAN RYAN

If people don't want to come out to the park, nobody's gonna stop 'em.   YOGI BERRA

To enjoy baseball, you do not need violence in your heart.

CHARLES EINSTEIN

I hit anything that's close to the plate. I don't wait for that one pitch.

ROD CAREW

BASKETBALL

I've got a theory that if you give 100 percent all of the time, somehow things will work out in the end.

LARRY BIRD

Nobody roots for Goliath.

WILT CHAMBERLAIN

Why be impressed by a basketball player unless there's something else about him you can admire?

DAVE COWENS

To be great we need to win games we aren't supposed to win.

JULIUS ERVING

Basketball is like war in that offensive weapons are developed first, and it always takes a while for the defense to catch up.

RED AUERBACH

If you're not on a great team, you don't get a chance to star.

JOHN WOODEN

If you don't have that big guy who can grab rebounds, you're dead.

BOB COUSY

If you lose the must game, the next one is a *really* must game.

EARL MONROE

If we win you will have a lot of free time; if we lose you belong to me.

RED HOLZMAN

BATTLE

Don't be a fool and die for your country. Let the other sonofabitch die for his.

GEORGE S. PATTON

Many men love to be in battle.

NORMAN MAILER

Usually a battle inclines in one direction from the very beginning, but in a manner hardly noticeable.

KARL VON CLAUSEWITZ

The quarters of an hour decide the issue of battle.

NAPOLEON BONAPARTE

No one who shuns the blows and the dust of battle wins a crown.

SAINT BASIL

If you want to win your battles, take an' work your bloomin' guns.

RUDYARD KIPLING

BEARD

The great ages of prose are the ages in which men shave. The great ages of poetry are those in which they allow their beards to grow.

ROBERT LYND

If you think that to grow a beard is to acquire wisdom, a goat is at once a complete Plato.   LUCIAN

It is easier to bear a child once a year than to shave every day.

RUSSIAN PROVERB

It contributes to a man's beauty, as a fine head of hair does to that of a woman.   SAINT CLEMENT OF ALEXANDRIA

Too many whiskers will spoil the broth.   FRANK RICHARDSON

Since we lost our beards we have no more souls.   SPANISH PROVERB

When a man shaves he announces it before and after. It is a great accomplishment and should not be underestimated.

MARCELENE COX

BEAUTY

Beauty? . . . To me it is a word without sense because I do not know where its meaning comes from nor where it leads to. PABLO PICASSO

Anyone who keeps the ability to see beauty never grows old.

FRANZ KAFKA

What is beautiful is moral; that is all there is to it.

GUSTAVE FLAUBERT

When we speak of beauty, we're speaking of something we're more or less indifferent to.   EDITH HAMILTON

I believe that one of the great problems for us as individuals is the depression and the tension resulting from existence in a world which is increasingly less pleasing to the eye.   LADY BIRD JOHNSON

After all, I suppose that all ugliness passes, and beauty endures, excepting of the skin.   EDITH SITWELL

When beauty seems to have abandoned the world, we must realize that it has first deserted our own hearts.   GEORGES DUHAMEL

Beauty itself doth of itself persuade the eyes of men without an orator.   SHAKESPEARE

Beauty is bread that never grows stale.   BRENDAN FRANCIS

It is the beautiful bird which gets caged.   CHINESE PROVERB

It may be that vice, depravity, and crime are nearly always, or even perhaps always, in their essence attempts to eat beauty, to eat what we should only look at.   SIMONE WEIL

The human soul needs actual beauty even more than bread.
D. H. LAWRENCE

BEAUTY, FEMALE

Beauty to no complexion is confined,
Is of all colours, and by none defined.
GEORGE GRANVILLE

Some of the most beautiful women I have ever met tell me, "I hate myself when I look in the mirror." I hear that again and again.
HENRY MILLER

It's better to be first with an ugly woman than the hundredth with a beauty.   PEARL BUCK

The new bold beauty is round; she's not scrawny. . . . Her body looks healthy, and strong enough so you could wrestle and roll with her.   FRANCESCO SCAVULLO

Perhaps if we lived with less physical beauty we would develop our true natures more.   SHIRLEY HAZZARD

There are no ugly women, only lazy ones.   HELENA RUBINSTEIN

Won't you come into the garden? I would like my roses to see you.
RICHARD B. SHERIDAN

The saying that beauty is but skin deep is but a skin deep saying.

JOHN RUSKIN

The most beautiful make-up of a woman is passion. But cosmetics are easier to buy.   YVES SAINT LAURENT

A woman who cannot be ugly is not beautiful.   KARL KRAUS

What, when drunk, one sees in other women, one sees in Garbo sober.   KENNETH TYNAN

The prettiest girl can give only what she has.   ALFRED DE MUSSET

People tell me some beauties lose their looks in bed when they don't do the bed things they're supposed to. I don't believe those things.   ANDY WARHOL

A mode of conduct, a standard of courage, discipline, fortitude, and integrity can do a great deal to make a woman beautiful.

JACQUELINE BISSET

BEGINNING

The only joy in the world is to begin.   CESARE PAVESE

The first step binds one to the second.   FRENCH PROVERB

Nothing, of course, begins at the time you think it did.

LILLIAN HELLMAN

There is no such thing as a long piece of work, except one that you dare not start.   CHARLES BAUDELAIRE

The great majority of men are bundles of beginnings.

RALPH WALDO EMERSON

The world is round and the place which may seem like the end may also be only the beginning.   IVY BAKER PRIEST

BELIEF

Face what you think you believe and you will be surprised.

WILLIAM HALE WHITE

A man can believe a considerable deal of rubbish, and yet go about his daily work in a rational and cheerful manner. NORMAN DOUGLAS

'Tis curious that we only believe as deeply as we live.

RALPH WALDO EMERSON

The only thing that is really difficult is to prove what one believes.

PAUL CÉZANNE

Some things have to be believed to be seen.   RALPH HODGSON

It is strange this life of men possessed with fervid beliefs that seem like madness to their fellow-beings.   GEORGE ELIOT

Few really believe. The most only believe that they believe or even make believe.   JOHN LANCASTER SPALDING

BEST

To get the best out of a man, go to what is best in him.

DANIEL CONSIDINE

We must never try to escape the obligation of living at our best.

JANET ERSKINE STUART

Even the best needles are not sharp at both ends. CHINESE PROVERB

What the best minds see to be no longer tenable will little by little lose its hold on the multitude also.   JOHN LANCASTER SPALDING

Every man is entitled to be valued by his best moments.

RALPH WALDO EMERSON

The best can never be within the reach of all.   JOHN A. LINCOLN

BIBLE

Why do they put the Gideon Bibles only in the bedrooms, where it's usually too late, and not in the barroom downstairs?

CHRISTOPHER MORLEY

It is only in Hebrew that you feel the full meaning of it—all the associations which a different word has.   DAVID BEN-GURION

You can learn more about human nature by reading the Bible than by living in New York.   WILLIAM LYON PHELPS

In the beginning, we had the land and the white man had the

Bible. Then we had the Bible and the white man had the land.

AFRICAN SAYING

The Bible may be the truth, but it is not the whole truth and nothing but the truth.   SAMUEL BUTLER

He rightly reads scripture who turns words into deeds.

SAINT BERNARD OF CLAIRVAUX

I have made it a practice for several years to read the Bible in the course of every year.   JOHN QUINCY ADAMS

Thousands have gone to heaven who never read one page of the Bible.   FRANCIS A. BAKER

The total absence of humor from the Bible is one of the most singular things in all literature.   ALFRED NORTH WHITEHEAD

In the Bible there is more that finds me than I have experienced in all other books put together.   SAMUEL TAYLOR COLERIDGE

The Bible has been the Magna Charta of the poor and oppressed.

THOMAS HENRY HUXLEY

BIRDS

A bird in the hand may soil your sleeve, but as long as you got the bird in there, you don't have to worry about where your next meal is coming from.   FRED ALLEN

No bird sits a tree more proudly than a pigeon. It looks as though placed there by the Lord.   KATHERINE MANSFIELD

The eagle never lost so much time as when he submitted to learn of the crow.   WILLIAM BLAKE

The dodo was (perverse distinction)
Immortalized by his extinction.

EDWARD LUCIE-SMITH

You know that if I were reincarnated, I'd want to come back a buzzard. Nothing hates him or envies him or wants him or needs him. He is never bothered . . . and he can eat anything.

WILLIAM FAULKNER

Caged birds accept each other but flight is what they long for.

TENNESSEE WILLIAMS

There is nothing in which the birds differ more from man than the way in which they can build and yet leave a landscape as it was before. ROBERT LYND

BLACK

I know a Southerner who owned an amusement park and almost went out of his mind over where to put us on a merry-go-round.

DICK GREGORY

The drums of Africa beat in my heart. They will not let me rest while there is a single Negro boy or girl without a chance to prove his worth. MARY MC LEOD BETHUNE

If a white man falls off a chair drunk, it's just a drunk. If a Negro does, it's the whole damn Negro race. BILL COSBY

The black American knows intuitively that his time of acceptance depends less on his own efforts than on the conscience of other ethnic groups who are affluent and secure and don't care to look behind them. WALTER CRONKITE

I think we Negro Americans have just as many beautiful people in mind and body, as well as skin, as any other group—and that we have just as many stinkers as any other group.

THURGOOD MARSHALL

We have been so patient and loyal.. . . and what has it gotten us? We want our full share now. SHIRLEY CHISHOLM

The trouble is that blacks are so visible. You hire one secretary and it looks like a lot of integration. WHITNEY M. YOUNG, JR.

To bring full justice and equality to black people is the historic assignment of this generation. We cannot evade that assignment and preserve the kind of nation we care about. JOHN W. GARDNER

It is clear that, for all the progress some of us have made, half of all black Americans are boat people without boats, cast adrift in a hostile ocean of discrimination, unemployment and poverty.

VERNON E. JORDAN, JR.

Our faith has been sorely tried, it has been burned in the furnace of racial hatreds, but always, black people have revived their faith in America and through their example and commitment, America's faith in itself. VERNON E. JORDAN, JR.

BLAME

There is luxury in self-reproach. . . . When we blame ourselves we feel no one else has a right to blame us.   OSCAR WILDE

There can be no doubt that the average man blames much more than he praises.   ARNOLD BENNETT

Our culture peculiarly honors the act of blaming, which it takes as the sign of virtue and intellect.   LIONEL TRILLING

Whatever you blame, that you have done yourself.
                                        GEORG GRODDECK

He who wants to blame sometimes finds the sugar sour.
                                        GERMAN PROVERB

The most disturbing and wasteful emotions in modern life, next to fright, are those which are associated with the idea of blame, directed against the self or against others.   HARVEY FERGUSSON

BODY

Darling, the only way to make the body more beautiful is to get a good man.   ZSA ZSA GABOR

Lovely female shapes are terrible complicators of the difficulties and dangers of this earthly life, especially for their owners.
                                        GEORGE DU MAURIER

Blood is that fragile scarlet tree we carry within us.
                                        SIR OSBERT SITWELL

Our own physical body possesses a wisdom which we who inhabit the body lack. We give it orders which make no sense.
                                        HENRY MILLER

Volumes are now being written and spoken about the effect of the mind on the body—I wish more was thought of the effect of the body on the mind.   FLORENCE NIGHTINGALE

Curve: The loveliest distance between two points.   MAE WEST

The word arse is as much god as the word face. It must be so, otherwise you cut off your god at the waist.   D. H. LAWRENCE

A woman with any sort of figure is prouder of it than a man is of a million dollars.   E. W. HOWE

The body is a big sagacity, a plurality with one sense, a war and a peace, a flock and a shepherd.   FRIEDRICH NIETZSCHE

The man who is so painstakingly cautious about doing his own body no harm seldom does anything for anyone else.   E. V. LUCAS

Language which does not acknowledge the body cannot acknowledge life.   JOHN LAHR

To a discerning and sensitive eye, a bottom shows character as clearly as a face, for the whole organism is manifested in every one of its features.   ALAN WATTS

A fat woman is a quilt for the winter.   PUNJABI PROVERB

The most popular image of the female despite the exigencies of the clothing trade is all boobs and buttocks, a hallucinating sequence of parabolae and bulges.   GERMAINE GREER

We have so many words for states of mind, and so few for the states of the body.   JEANNE MOREAU

BOLDNESS

It is better to be bold than too circumspect, because fortune is of a sex which likes not a tardy wooer and repulses all who are not ardent.   MACHIAVELLI

Fortune and Love befriend the bold.   OVID

It is the fact, that by the constitution of society, the bold, the vigorous, and the buoyant rise and rule; and that the weak, the shrinking, and the timid fall and serve.   WALTER BAGEHOT

Fear created gods; boldness created kings.   PROSPER JALYOT

Put a grain of boldness into everything you do.   BALTASAR GRACIAN

BOOKS

The success of many books is due to the affinity between the mediocrity of the author's ideas and those of the public.
NICHOLAS DE CHAMFORT

Books are no substitute for living, but they can add immeasurably to its richness.   MAY HILL ARBUTHNOT

A book is a mirror: When a monkey looks in, no apostle can look out.   GEORGE C. LICHTENBERG

I love the place; the magnificent books; I require books as I require air.   SHOLEM ASCH

There is no remedy so easy as books, which if they do not give cheerfulness, at least restore quiet to the most troubled mind.
                         LADY MARY WORTLEY MONTAGU

There is a great deal of difference between an eager man who wants to read a book and the tired man who wants a book to read.
                                    G. K. CHESTERTON

The man who does not read good books has no advantage over the man who can't read them.   MARK TWAIN

Books are not made for furniture, but there is nothing else that so beautifully furnishes a house.   HENRY WARD BEECHER

Many books require no thought from those who read them, and for a very simple reason. They made no such demand upon those who wrote them.   CHARLES CALEB COLTON

We really learn only from books we cannot judge. The author of a book we were able to evaluate should learn from us.   GOETHE

There are many little ways to enlarge [your child's] world. Love of books is the best of all.   JACQUELINE KENNEDY

BORE

Bore: A man who deprives you of solitude without providing you with company.   GIAN VINCENZO GRAVINA

We are all bores in certain uncongenial social climates: all stars in our own particular milky way.   RICHARD LE GALLIENNE

The secret of being a bore is to tell everything.   VOLTAIRE

Really, I'm a square. But it's the squares who carry the burden of the world, and the bores who become heroes.   KATHARINE HEPBURN

It is a tolerable depiction of a bore that he is one who talks about himself when you want to talk about yourself.
                                ROBERT HUGH BENSON

Some people are so boring that they make you waste an entire day in five minutes.   JULES RENARD

Bores are good too. They may help you to a good indignation, if not to a sympathy.   RALPH WALDO EMERSON

We all denounce bores, but while we do so, let us remember that there is nobody who isn't a bore to somebody.   J. A. SPENDER

There is no bore we dread being left alone with so much as our own minds.   JAMES RUSSELL LOWELL

BOREDOM

Boredom is an emptiness filled with insistence.   LEO STEIN

The average male gets his living by such depressing devices that boredom becomes a sort of natural state to him.   H. L. MENCKEN

Boredom flourishes too, when you feel safe. It's a symptom of security.   EUGENE IONESCO

Boredom is a vital problem for the moralist, since at least half the sins of mankind are caused by the fear of it.   BERTRAND RUSSELL

Boredom: The desire for desires.   LEO TOLSTOY

One can be bored until boredom becomes the most sublime of all emotions.   LOGAN PEARSALL SMITH

The war between being and nothingness is the underlying illness of the twentieth century. Boredom slays more of existence than war.
                                                    NORMAN MAILER

Nobody is bored when he is trying to make something that is beautiful, or to discover something that is true.   WILLIAM R. INGE

I do not get my ideas from people on the street. If you look at faces on the street, what do you see? Nothing, just boredom.
                                                    MARCEL MARCEAU

Boredom is the bitter fruit of too much routine or none at all.
                                                    BRENDAN FRANCIS

A friend asked Alexandre Dumas, who had just returned from a dinner party, whether he hadn't been bored. "I should have been," replied Dumas, "if I hadn't been there."

BOXING

I believe in being gentle and knocking 'em out clean with a good punch on the right spot.   BOB FITZSIMMONS

Boxing is sort of like jazz. The better it is the less amount of people can appreciate it.   GEORGE FOREMAN

A champion owes everybody something. He can never pay back for all the help he got, for making him an idol.   JACK DEMPSEY

I do but little boxing because it seems rather absurd for a president to appear with a black eye or a swollen nose or a cut lip.
                                              THEODORE ROOSEVELT

Yes, I was fond of *les jeunes filles.* I liked to have a new girl once a week when I was training for a fight.   GEORGES CARPENTIER

Few lapses of self-control are punished as immediately and severely as loss of temper during a boxing bout.   KONRAD LORENZ

The fundamental appeal lies in watching one guy try to knock another guy's block off.   ROBERT LIPSYTE

Don't ever match a bull against a master boxer. The bull is stronger but the matador is smarter.   MUHAMMAD ALI

I was a little bit sore at Schmeling for some of the things he said; but no, I ain't going over to see him at the hospital.   JOE LOUIS

The greatest barroom fighter who, I assume, can be termed a natural fighter could not possibly cope with the poorest fourth-rate professional.   GENE TUNNEY

When going into the ring I have always had it in mind that I would be the conqueror. That has always been my disposition.
                                                JOHN L. SULLIVAN

Cruelty and absolute lack of mercy are essential qualities in every successful prizefighter.   PAUL GALLICO

A good fighter usually knows, to within a very few seconds, when a three-minute round is going to end.   JACK DEMPSEY

Unless you've been in the ring when the noise is for you, there's no way you'll ever know what it's like.   SUGAR RAY ROBINSON

BREASTS

A woman without breasts is like a bed without pillows.

ANATOLE FRANCE

There's an extraordinary difference between a beautiful nipple and a dull one.   NORMAN MAILER

If I hadn't had them, I would have had some made. DOLLY PARTON

The most highly prized curve of all is that of the bosom.

GERMAINE GREER

The reason why the bosom of a beautiful woman is an object of such peculiar delight arises from hence: that all our first pleasurable sensations of warmth, sustenance, and repose are derived from this interesting source.   CHARLES CALEB COLTON

> Gaze on her bosom of sweets, and take
>   This truth for a constant rule:—
> Enchanting woman can always make
>   The wisest of men a fool.

GEORGE COLMAN

BROTHERHOOD

On this shrunken globe, men can no longer live as strangers.

ADLAI E. STEVENSON

Tolerance is good for all, or it is good for none.   EDMUND BURKE

You cannot contribute anything to the ideal condition of mind and heart known as Brotherhood, however much you preach, posture, or agree, unless you live it.   FAITH BALDWIN

This whole striving for brotherhood is somehow in the very nature of things. Once you affirm it, you're in the stream of existence.

ROBERT C. POLLOCK

Every bigot was once a child free of prejudice.

SISTER MARY DE LOURDES

The achievement of brotherhood is the crowning objective of our society.   DWIGHT D. EISENHOWER

To know that all men are brothers is not only to know that all men are alike, but, more important, to know that all men are different.

ROBERT W. BURNS

To him in whom love dwells, the whole world is but one family.

BUDDHA

We didn't all come over on the same ship, but we're all in the same boat.   BERNARD M. BARUCH

I look to a time when brotherhood needs no publicity; to a time when a brotherhood award would be as ridiculous as an award for getting up each morning.   DANIEL D. MICH

In the final analysis our most common basic link is that we all inhabit this small planet. We all breathe the same air. We all cherish our children's future. And we are all mortal.   JOHN F. KENNEDY

Each of us depends on the rest of mankind for the bare fact of survival.   EMMANUEL CARDINAL SUHARD

BUSINESS

Business is a combination of war and sport.   ANDRÉ MAUROIS

The trouble with senior management to an outsider is that there are too many one-ulcer men holding down two-ulcer jobs.

PRINCE PHILIP

The secret of business is to know something that nobody else knows.   ARISTOTLE ONASSIS

I resent large corporations. They flatten personalities.

BOB NEWHART

Live together like brothers and do business like strangers.

ARAB PROVERB

It is just as important that business keep out of government as that government keep out of business.   HERBERT HOOVER

Business is more agreeable than pleasure; it interests the whole mind, the aggregate nature of man more continuously and more deeply. But it does not *look* as if it did.   WALTER BAGEHOT

When two men in business always agree, one of them is unnecessary.   WILLIAM WRIGLEY, JR.

Offices are a tremendous waste of time for chief executives. . . . I can be away from my office for three weeks, and things get done. But if I come in for one day, everything stops. LAWRENCE A. APPLY

Business is never so healthy as when, like a chicken, it must do a certain amount of scratching for what it gets.   HENRY FORD

Anybody can cut prices, but it takes brains to make a better article.   ALICE HUBBARD

The commercial man almost has to be a romanticist because he so often deals with unrealities.   G. K. CHESTERTON

CALIFORNIA

California: A state that's washed by the Pacific on one side and cleaned by Las Vegas on the other.   AL COOPER

Symbolically, California means to me a person walking by a highway alone while everybody else goes by in a car.   GLORIA STEINEM

I attended a dinner the other morning for the Old Settlers in California. No one was allowed to attend unless he had been in the state two and one half years.   WILL ROGERS

My friend Max Reinhardt has a house in California. . . . The skies are a heavenly blue. It is a part of your great country that is very much alive.   THOMAS MANN

In California I find people have the same psychology about marriage as they do about buying a house. . . . When they go into a house, they're already thinking of the next one.   CONNIE STEVENS

Even when Californians head toward the desert, they do so more to marvel at the presence of swimming pools and fountains than to play in the sand.   JESSAMYN WEST

CANDOR

We talk plainly only to those we love. JEAN BAPTISTE LACORDAIRE

Candor is always a double-edged sword; it may heal or it may separate.   DR. WILHELM STEKEL

A man that should call everything by its right name would hardly pass the streets without being knocked down as a common enemy.

LORD HALIFAX

If you want to get rid of somebody, just tell 'em something for their own good.   KIN HUBBARD

If one says what he thinks, the other too says what he thinks.

CHARLES PÉGUY

The man who says what he thinks is finished and the man who thinks what he says is an idiot.   ROLF HOCKMUTH

CARING

A generous heart feels others' ills as if it were responsible for them.

VAUVENARGUES

Each of us is a being in himself and a being in society, each of us needs to understand himself and understand others, take care of others and be taken care of himself.   HANIEL LONG

Caring is everything; nothing matters but caring.
The last words of BARON FRIEDRICH VON HUGEL

Too many of us stay walled up because we are afraid of being hurt. We are afraid to care too much, for fear that the other person does not care at all.   ELEANOR ROOSEVELT

I never ask the wounded person how he feels; I myself become the wounded person.   WALT WHITMAN

CAT

Cats seem to go on the principle that it never does any harm to ask for what you want.   JOSEPH WOOD KRUTCH

Of all God's creatures there is only one that cannot be made the slave of the lash. That one is the cat.   MARK TWAIN

No favor can win gratitude from a cat.   LA FONTAINE

The cat is the only animal without visible means of support who still manages to find a living in the city.   CARL VAN VECHTEN

It is in his own interest that the cat purrs.   IRISH PROVERB

It is easy to guess why the rabble dislike cats. A cat is beautiful; it suggests ideas of luxury, cleanliness, voluptuous pleasures . . . etc.
CHARLES BAUDELAIRE

> Sally, having swallowed cheese
> Directs down holes the scented breeze
> Enticing thus with bated breath,
> Nice mice to an untimely death.
>
> GEOFFREY TAYLOR

Cat: A pygmy lion who loves mice, hates dogs, and patronizes human beings.   OLIVER HERFORD

It is in the nature of cats to do a certain amount of roaming. . . . To escort a cat abroad on a leash is against the nature of the owner.
ADLAI E. STEVENSON,
message to Illinois Senate, April 23, 1949

CAUSE

It is a common error to imagine that to be stirring and voluble in a worthy cause is to be good and to do good.
JOHN LANCASTER SPALDING

A bad cause requires many words.   GERMAN PROVERB

None know what it is to live till they redeem life from its seeming monotony by laying it a sacrifice on the altar of some great cause.
WENDELL PHILLIPS

Faith in a holy cause is to a considerable extent a substitute for the lost faith in ourselves.   ERIC HOFFER

We all are ready to be savage in some cause. The difference between a good man and a bad one is the choice of the cause.
WILLIAM JAMES

CENSORSHIP

I never knew a girl who was ruined by a book.   JAMES J. WALKER

Censors are pretty sure to be fools.   JAMES HARVEY ROBINSON

With the abolition of censorship, anything goes now. As a result we get the worst, artistically speaking, in all the media. HENRY MILLER

Only the suppressed word is dangerous.   LUDWIG BORNE

The censor-moron does not really hate anything but the living and growing human consciousness.   D. H. LAWRENCE

Censorship reflects society's lack of confidence in itself. It is a hall-mark of an authoritarian regime.   POTTER STEWART

CERTAINTY

In these matters the only certainty is that there is nothing certain.
PLINY THE ELDER

Certitude is not the test of certainty. We have been cocksure of many things that were not so.   OLIVER WENDELL HOLMES, JR.

Love of certainty is a demand for guarantees in advance of action.
JOHN DEWEY

There is only one thing about which I am certain, and this is that there is very little about which one can be certain.
W. SOMERSET MAUGHAM

We can be absolutely certain only about things we do not under-stand.   ERIC HOFFER

CHANCE

Chance is always powerful, let your hook always be cast; in the pool where you least expect it, there will be a fish.   OVID

He that leaveth nothing to chance will do very few things ill, but he will do very few things.   LORD HALIFAX

How often events, by chance, and unexpectedly, came to pass, which you had not dared even to hope for!   TERENCE

Experience has proved that chance is often as much concerned in deciding . . . matters as bravery; and always more than the justice of the cause.   GEORGE WASHINGTON

CHANGE

To blind oneself to change is not therefore to halt it.

ISAAC GOLDBERG

It isn't so much that hard times are coming; the change observed is mostly soft times going.   GROUCHO MARX

It is in the nature of a man as he grows older . . . to protest against change, particularly change for the better.   JOHN STEINBECK

The healthy being craves an occasional wildness, a jolt from normality, a sharpening of the edge of appetite, his own little festival of the Saturnalia, a brief excursion from his way of life.

ROBERT MAC IVER

Someday perhaps change will occur when times are ready for it instead of always when it is too late. Someday change will be accepted as life itself.   SHIRLEY MAC LAINE

I think anything you try to do to change anything, even if you explain it to them, the majority of people object.

PHILIP K. WRIGLEY

The circumstances of the world are so variable that an irrevocable purpose or opinion is almost synonymous with a foolish one.

WILLIAM H. SEWARD

If you want to make enemies, try to change something.

WOODROW WILSON

The wheel of change moves on, and those who were down go up and those who were up go down.   JAWAHARLAL NEHRU

Some things, of course, you can't change. Pretending that you have is like painting stripes on a horse and hollering "Zebra!"

EDDIE CANTOR

Only that which is provisional endures.   FRENCH PROVERB

The feminine desire to matchmake, either for oneself or others, the hankering to change a thing, whether it be a man or a job or a cook or the curtains, does not die with matrimony. Usually it only dies with the lady.   ILKA CHASE

CHARACTER

There is nothing so fatal to character as half-finished tasks.

DAVID LLOYD GEORGE

When a man thinks he is reading the character of another, he is often unconsciously betraying his own.   JOSEPH FARRELL

To judge a man's character by only one of its manifestations is like judging the sea by a jugful of its water.   PAUL ELDRIDGE

If a man has character, he also has his typical experience, which always recurs.   FRIEDRICH NIETZSCHE

Some people strengthen the society just by being the kind of people they are.   JOHN W. GARDNER

If you hear that a mountain has moved, believe; but if you hear that a man has changed his character, believe it not.

MOHAMMEDAN PROVERB

Persons with weight of character carry, like planets, their atmospheres along with them in their orbits.   THOMAS HARDY

I forgot that every little action of the common day makes or unmakes character, and that therefore what one has done in the secret chamber one has some day to cry aloud on the house-tops.

OSCAR WILDE

I begin to find that too good a character is inconvenient.

SIR WALTER SCOTT

The universe seems bankrupt as soon as we begin to discuss the characters of individuals.   HENRY DAVID THOREAU

Underneath this flabby exterior is an enormous lack of character.

OSCAR LEVANT

CHARM

A woman of charm is as rare as a man of genius.

SALVADOR DE MADARIAGA

If a person has charm he never loses it; and charm never fatigues.

ANDRÉ MAUROIS

It is absurd to divide people into good and bad. People are either charming or tedious.   OSCAR WILDE

A beauty is a woman you notice; a charmer is one who notices you.
                                                    ADLAI E. STEVENSON

Modesty is the gentle art of enhancing your charm by pretending not to be aware of it.   OLIVER HERFORD

The basic thing which contributes to charm is the ability to forget oneself and be engrossed in other people.   ELEANOR ROOSEVELT

CHASTITY

A woman's chastity consists, like an onion, of a series of coats.
                                                 NATHANIEL HAWTHORNE

Chastity is the lily among virtues and makes men almost equal to angels.   SAINT FRANCIS DE SALES

Chastity is perhaps the most peculiar of all sexual aberrations.
                                                    REMY DE GOURMONT

Chastity is a virtue with some, but with many almost a vice. These are continent to be sure; but doggish lust looketh enviously out of all that they do.   FRIEDRICH NIETZSCHE

The very ice of chastity is in them.   SHAKESPEARE

A woman's honor is concerned with one thing only, and it is a thing with which the honor of a man is not concerned at all.
                                                  JAMES BRANCH CABELL

CHILDREN

I must have been an insufferable child; all children are.
                                                 GEORGE BERNARD SHAW

Small children disturb your sleep, big children your life.
                                                    YIDDISH PROVERB

There is no possible method.of compelling a child to feel sympathy or affection.   BERTRAND RUSSELL

My object will be, if possible, to form Christian men, for Christian boys I can scarcely hope to make.   THOMAS ARNOLD,
on appointment to the headmastership of Rugby

What the best and wisest parent wants for his own child that must be what the community wants for all its children.   JOHN DEWEY

Parents learn a lot from their children about coping with life.
                                                        MURIEL SPARK

Children are natural mimics—they act like their parents in spite of every attempt to teach them good manners.   ANONYMOUS

Children are likely to live up to what you believe of them.
                                                  LADY BIRD JOHNSON

There's no such thing as a tough child—if you parboil them first for seven hours, they always come out tender.   W. C. FIELDS

A child's house of its own is the wide outside accessible to it at any time. Anywhere away from its parents.   SYLVIA ASHTON-WARNER

If any of us had a child that we thought was as bad as we know we are, we would have cause to start to worry.   WILL ROGERS

It is dangerous to confuse children with angels.
                                            SIR DAVID MAXWELL FYFE

When people want children to be romanticized, they apply to bachelors.   OSCAR W. FIRKINS

Grown-ups never understand anything for themselves, and it is tiresome for children to be always and forever explaining things to them.   ANTOINE DE SAINT-EXUPÉRY

She never quite leaves her children at home, even when she doesn't take them along.   MARGARET CULKIN BANNING

CHRISTIANITY

Christianity is not being destroyed by the confusions and concussions of the time; it is being discovered.   HUGH E. BROWN

A great deal of what passes for current Christianity consists in denouncing other people's vices and faults.
                                          MSGR. HENRY H. WILLIAMS

If Christianity has never disturbed us, we have not yet learned
what it is.   WILLIAM TEMPLE

Christianity, the gentlest of religious professions, is the most mili-
tant and warlike of religions, the most successful and Faustian of
religions. Indeed, it conquered the world.   NORMAN MAILER

Scratch the Christian and you find the pagan—spoiled.
                                                   ISRAEL ZANGWILL

Christian ethics are seldom found save in the philosophy of some
unbeliever.   HEYWOOD HALE BROUN

There is no greater and more dangerous enemy of Christianity
than all that makes it small and narrow.   ABBÉ HUVELIN

Christianity inclines us to do all the good we can without too close
scrutiny into persons and things.   MSGR. MARTIN J. SPALDING

Christianity gave Eros poison to drink. Eros did not die of it, to be
sure, but degenerated into vice.   FRIEDRICH NIETZSCHE

CHRISTMAS

Christmas is not a date. It is a state of mind.   MARY ELLEN CHASE

I can understand people simply fleeing the mountainous effort
Christmas has become . . . but there are always a few saving graces
and finally they make up for all the bother and distress.
                                                   MAY SARTON

Nothing's as mean as giving a little child something useful for
Christmas.   KIN HUBBARD

The Christmas season has come to mean the period when the public plays Santa Claus to the merchants.   JOHN ANDREW HOLMES

There is always somebody that one is afraid not to give a Christmas present to.   ANONYMOUS

Isn't it funny that at Christmas something in you gets so lonely
for—I don't know what exactly, but it's something that you don't
mind so much not having at other times.   KATE L. BOSHER

The season always gives me the blues in spite of myself, though I manage to get a good deal of pleasure from thinking of the multi-tudes of happy kids in various parts of the world.

EDWIN ARLINGTON ROBINSON

The things we do at Christmas are touched with a certain extrava-gance, as beautiful, in some of its aspects, as the extravagance of Nature in June.   ROBERT COLLYER

CIRCUMSTANCES

Man's highest merit always is, as much as possible, to rule external circumstances and as little as possible to let himself be ruled by them.   GOETHE

I am unfaithful to my own possibilities when I await from a change of circumstances what I can do on my own initiative.

KARL JASPERS

All of us have wonders hidden in our breasts, only needing circum-stances to evoke them.   CHARLES DICKENS

It always remains true that if we had been greater, circumstances would have been less strong against us.   GEORGE ELIOT

As the water shapes itself to the vessel that contains it, so a wise man adapts himself to circumstances.   CONFUCIUS

CITY

Despite the litany of the sorrows of the city, we must believe in the ability of man to respond to the problems of his environment.

CARL B. STOKES

No city should be too large for a man to walk out of in a morning.

CYRIL CONNOLLY

There are natures that go to the streams of life in great cities as the hart goes to the water brooks.   PHILIP G. HAMERTON

A mayor must be a sack of concrete. They come in all day, every day, and beat at you with baseball bats.   JOSEPH M. BARR,
former mayor of Pittsburgh

Cities are full of people with whom a certain degree of contact is useful and enjoyable, but you do not want them in your hair. And they do not want you in theirs either.   JANE JACOBS

A large city cannot be experientially known; its life is too manifold for any individual to be able to participate in it.   ALDOUS HUXLEY

The typical American city is in fragments—a variety of worlds wholly out of touch with each other.   JOHN W. GARDNER

CIVILIZATION

In a world flagrant with the failures of civilization, what is there particularly immortal about our own?   G. K. CHESTERTON

It must be admitted that there is a degree of instability which is inconsistent with civilization. But, on the whole, the great ages have been unstable ages.   ALFRED NORTH WHITEHEAD

Every civilization is, among other things, an arrangement for domesticating the passions and setting them to do useful work.

ALDOUS HUXLEY

Civilization is unbearable, but it is *less* unbearable at the top.

TIMOTHY LEARY

Civilized men arrived in the Pacific, armed with alcohol, syphilis, treasures, and the Bible.   HAVELOCK ELLIS

Civilization is a movement and not a condition, a voyage and not a harbor.   ARNOLD TOYNBEE

CLOTHES

Women who are not vain about their clothes are often vain about not being vain about their clothes.   CYRIL SCOTT

I have a hankering to go back to the Orient and discard my necktie. Neckties strangle clear thinking.   LIN YUTANG

What a man most enjoys about a woman's clothes are his fantasies of how she would look without them.   BRENDAN FRANCIS

Brevity is the soul of lingerie.   DOROTHY PARKER

I've really tried to learn the art of clothes, because you don't sell for what you're worth unless you look well.   LADY BIRD JOHNSON

Mink coat: A woman's reward for indifference.   OSCAR LEVANT

I don't know of nothing better'n a woman if you want to spend money where it'll show.   KIN HUBBARD

It is an interesting question how far men would retain their relative rank if they were divested of their clothes.
HENRY DAVID THOREAU

A skirt is no obstacle to extemporaneous sex, but it is physically impossible to make love to a girl while she is wearing trousers.
HELEN LAWRENSON

It is about as stupid to let your clothes betray that you know you are ugly as to have them proclaim that you know you are beautiful.   EDITH WHARTON

Slacks are becoming only to very slim figures.
ELEANOR ROOSEVELT

Every time a woman leaves off something she looks better, but every time a man leaves off something he looks worse.
WILL ROGERS

Women are latent exhibitionists. They love to wear things that attract masculine attention, even if the getups are crazy.
ERLE STANLEY GARDNER

It is remarkable how great an influence our clothes have on our moral state.   ANATOLE FRANCE

Nowadays if men are more serious than women, it's because their clothes are darker.   ANDRÉ GIDE

COLD, COMMON

Like everybody else, when I don't know what else to do, I seem to go in for catching colds.   GEORGE JEAN NATHAN

A cold is both positive and negative; sometimes the Eyes have it and sometimes the Nose.   WILLIAM LYON PHELPS

Why is it that men who can go through severe accidents, air raids, and any other major crisis always seem to think they are at death's door when they have a simple head cold?   SHIRLEY BOOTH

A bad cold wouldn't be so annoying if it weren't for the advice of our friends.   KIN HUBBARD

COMMITTEE

We always carry out by committee anything in which any one of us alone would be too reasonable to persist.   FRANK MOORE COLBY

I said what is very true, that any committee is only as good as the most knowledgeable, determined, and vigorous person on it. There must be somebody who provides the flame.   LADY BIRD JOHNSON

I think a single man can accomplish in a day what a committee could accomplish in a month.   BILL LEAR

A committee is a group of men who, individually, can do nothing, but collectively can meet and decide that nothing can be done.   ANONYMOUS

I hate being placed on committees. They are always having meetings at which half are absent and the rest late.   OLIVER WENDELL HOLMES, JR.

COMPLAINT

We mourn the transitory things and fret under the yoke of the immutable ones.   PAUL ELDRIDGE

I think that the insane desire one has sometimes to bang and kick grumblers and peevish persons is a Divine instinct.   ROBERT HUGH BENSON

Complain to one who can help you.   YUGOSLAV PROVERB

It is a great imperfection to complain unceasingly of little things.   SAINT FRANCIS DE SALES

Oh, wouldn't the world seem dull and flat with nothing whatever to grumble at?   W. S. GILBERT

Every man may be observed to have a certain strain of lamentation, some peculiar theme of complaint, on which he dwells in his moments of dejection.   SAMUEL JOHNSON

Obtain from yourself all that makes complaining useless. No longer implore from others what you yourself can obtain.

ANDRÉ GIDE

COMPLIMENT

The compliment that helps us on our way is not the one that is shut up in the mind, but the one that is spoken out.   MARK TWAIN

Some folks pay a compliment like they went down in their pocket for it.   KIN HUBBARD

Of a compliment only a third is meant.   WELSH PROVERB

In vain do people say good things of us, for we think so many more.   J. PETIT-SENN

Women are never disarmed by compliments, men always are.

OSCAR WILDE

CONCENTRATION

For him who has no concentration, there is no tranquillity.

BHAGAVAD GITA

The real essence of work is concentrated energy . . . people who really have that in a superior degree by nature are independent of the forms and habits and artifices by which less able and active people are kept up to their labors.   WALTER BAGEHOT

One of the most important factors—not only in military matters but in life as a whole—is the power of execution, the ability to direct one's whole energies toward the fulfillment of a particular task.   ERWIN ROMMEL

If you would be pope, you must think of nothing else.

SPANISH PROVERB

CONDUCT

Life, not the parson, teaches conduct.

OLIVER WENDELL HOLMES, JR.

The superior man is slow in his words and earnest in his conduct.

CONFUCIUS

I don't never have any trouble in regulating my own conduct, but to keep other folks' straight is what bothers me.   JOSH BILLINGS

The ultimate test for us of what a truth means is the conduct it dictates or inspires.   WILLIAM JAMES

I am a firm believer in the theory that the strongest motive, whether we are conscious of it or not, rules our conduct.

ELLEN GLASGOW

CONFIDENCE

Jimmy taught me a long time ago that you do the best you can and don't worry about the criticisms. Once you accept the fact that you're not perfect, then you develop some confidence.

ROSALYNN CARTER

It is best in the theatre to act with confidence no matter how little right you have to it.   LILLIAN HELLMAN

Be humble, for the worst thing in the world is of the same stuff as you; be confident, for the stars are of the same stuff as you.

NICHOLAI VELIMIROVIC

When I went duck hunting with Bear Bryant, he shot at one but it kept flying. "John," he said, "there flies a dead duck." Now, that's confidence.   JOHN MC KAY

Confidence in another's integrity is no slight evidence of one's own.

MONTAIGNE

You must not have too much fear of not being up to your task when you are approaching great problems and great works.

GEORGES DUHAMEL

Confidence always gives pleasure to the man in whom it is placed.

LA ROCHEFOUCAULD

CONFORMITY

I have to live for others and not for myself; that's middle-class morality.   GEORGE BERNARD SHAW

We are half ruined by conformity; but we should be wholly ruined without it.   CHARLES DUDLEY WARNER

Success, recognition, and conformity are the bywords of the modern world where everyone seems to crave the anesthetizing security of being identified with the majority.   MARTIN LUTHER KING, JR.

Our society cannot have it both ways: to maintain a conformist and ignoble system *and* to have skillful and spirited men to man that system with.   PAUL GOODMAN

What is it about us, the public, and what is it about conformity itself that causes us all to require it of our neighbors and of our artists and then, with consummate fickleness, to forget those who fall into line and eternally celebrate those who do not? BEN SHAHN

A man must consider what a rich realm he abdicates when he becomes a conformist.   RALPH WALDO EMERSON

To think for himself! Oh, my God, teach him to think like other people!   MARY WOLLSTONECRAFT SHELLEY (1797–1851),
                    on being advised to send her son to a school
                    where he would be taught to think for himself

Trumpet in a herd of elephants; crow in the company of cocks; bleat in a flock of goats.   MALAY PROVERB

CONSCIENCE

The man who acts never has any conscience; no one has any conscience but the man who thinks.   GOETHE

If we cannot be happy and powerful and prey on others, we invent conscience and prey on ourselves.   ELBERT HUBBARD

To most men, conscience is an occasional, almost an external voice.   WALTER BAGEHOT

Conscience whispers, but interest screams aloud.   J. PETIT-SENN

We grow with years more fragile in body, but morally stouter, and can throw off the chill of a bad conscience almost at once.
                                           LOGAN PEARSALL SMITH

Conscience is the inner voice that warns us somebody may be looking.   H. L. MENCKEN

Conscience gets a lot of credit that belongs to cold feet.

ANONYMOUS

CONSCIOUSNESS

Becoming conscious is of course a sacrilege against nature; it is as though you had robbed the unconscious of something.

CARL G. JUNG

The more you open your consciousness, the fewer unpleasant events intrude themselves into your awareness.   THADDEUS GOLAS

We can only be said to be alive in those moments when our hearts are conscious of our treasures.   THORNTON WILDER

If a man . . . asleep . . . wishes to awake, then everything that helps him to awake will be *good* and everything that hinders him . . . will be *evil*.   GEORGES GURDJIEFF

To be too conscious is an illness—a real thoroughgoing illness.

FYODOR DOSTOEVSKI

The mind has infinite stores beneath its present consciousness.

WILLIAM ELLERY CHANNING

CONTENTMENT

Those who are quite satisfied sit still and do nothing; those who are not quite satisfied are the sole benefactors of the world.

WALTER SAVAGE LANDOR

If everyone were satisfied, no one would buy the new thing.

CHARLES F. KETTERING

To live in quiet content is surely a piece of good citizenship.

GEORGE GISSING

Better a handful of dry dates and content therewith than to own the Gate of Peacocks and be kicked in the eye by a broody camel.

ARAB PROVERB

Be contented, when you have got all you want. HOLBROOK JACKSON

One should be either sad or joyful. Contentment is a warm sty for eaters and sleepers.   EUGENE O'NEILL

CONVERSATION

Well, many times I say only yes or no to people. Even that's too much. It winds them up for twenty minutes more.

CALVIN COOLDIGE

We'll talk without listening to each other; that is the best way to get along.   ALFRED DE MUSSET

He that says what he likes will hear what he doesna like.

SCOTTISH PROVERB

I am annoyed by individuals who are embarrassed by pauses in a conversation. To me, every conversational pause refreshes.

GEORGE SANDERS

I felt it shelter to speak to you.   EMILY DICKINSON

One way to prevent conversation from being boring is to say the wrong thing.   FRANK SHEED

Modest egotism is the salt of conversation; you do not want too much of it, but if it is altogether omitted, everything tastes flat.

HENRY VAN DYKE

No man would listen to you talk if he didn't know it was his turn next.   E. W. HOWE

Two great talkers will not travel far together.   GEORGE BORROW

The essential charm of good talking rests upon sincerity, spontaneity, and the willing revelation of character.   JOHN OLIVER HOBBES

COOKING

The only real stumbling block is fear of failure. In cooking you've got to have a what-the-hell attitude.   JULIA CHILD

Men make better cooks than women because they put so much more feeling into it.   MYRTLE REED

Occasional examples of bad temper are inevitable in the case of men and women cooks.   SAINT VINCENT DE PAUL

Cooking is like love. It should be entered into with abandon or not at all.   HARRIET VAN HORNE

All cooking is a matter of time. In general, the more time the better.   JOHN ERSKINE

Be content to remember that those who can make omelettes properly can do nothing else.   HILAIRE BELLOC

To the old saying that man built the house but woman made of it a "home" might be added the modern supplement that woman accepted cooking as a chore but man has made of it a recreation.

EMILY POST

A good cook is like a sorceress who dispenses happiness.

ELSA SCHIAPARELLI

COUNTRY LIFE

I have no relish for the country; it is a kind of healthy grave.

SYDNEY SMITH

I lived in solitude in the country and noticed how the monotony of a quiet life stimulates the creative mind.   ALBERT EINSTEIN

Our first parents lived in the country, and they promptly committed the only sin they were given a chance to commit.

AGNES REPPLIER

Very few people who have settled entirely in the country, but have grown at length weary of one another.

LADY MARY WORTLEY MONTAGU

It is only in the country that we can get to know a person or a book.   CYRIL CONNOLLY

A man's soul may be buried and perish under a dungheap or in a furrow of the field, just as well as under a pile of money.

NATHANIEL HAWTHORNE

Those who never sink into this peace of nature lose a tremendous well of strength, for there is something healing and life-giving in the mere atmosphere surrounding a country house.

ELEANOR ROOSEVELT

I suppose the pleasure of country life lies really in the eternally renewed evidences of the determination to live.

VITA SACKVILLE-WEST

A hick town is one where there is no place to go where you shouldn't be.   ALEXANDER WOOLLCOTT

COURAGE

What is more mortifying than to feel you've missed the Plum for want of courage to shake the Tree?   LOGAN PEARSALL SMITH

Any dangerous spot is tenable if brave men will make it so.
JOHN F. KENNEDY

Tell a man he is brave, and you help him to become so.
THOMAS CARLYLE

We learn courageous action by going forward whenever fear urges us back. A little boy was asked how he learned to skate. "Oh, by getting up every time I fell down," he answered.   DAVID SEABURY

Men who have lost heart never yet won a trophy.   GREEK PROVERB

No one has yet computed how many imaginary triumphs are silently celebrated by people each year to keep up their courage.
HENRY S. HASKINS

Depend upon it, the brave man has somehow or other to give his life away.   THOMAS CARLYLE

It gives one a sense of freedom to know that anyone in this world can really do a deliberately courageous act.   HENRIK IBSEN

Courage is as often the outcome of despair as of hope; in the one case we have nothing to lose, in the other everything to gain.
DIANE DE POITIERS

Courage is the basic virtue for everyone so long as he continues to grow, to move ahead.   ROLLO MAY

Many women miss their greatest chance of happiness through a want of courage in the decisive moments of their lives.
WINIFRED GORDON

What would life be if we had no courage to attempt anything?
VINCENT VAN GOGH

Courage is rightly esteemed the first of human qualities . . . because it is the quality which guarantees all others.
SIR WINSTON CHURCHILL

COURTESY

Whoever one is, and wherever one is, one is always in the wrong if one is rude.   MAURICE BARING

Good manners and soft words have brought many a difficult thing to pass.   SIR JOHN VANBRUGH

Politeness is not always the sign of wisdom, but the want of it always leaves room for the suspicion of folly.

WALTER SAVAGE LANDOR

Polished brass will pass upon more people than rough gold.

LORD CHESTERFIELD

A gentleman is simply a patient wolf.   LANA TURNER

Rudeness is the weak man's imitation of strength.   ERIC HOFFER

It is incredible what a difference it makes to one's feelings towards the whole human race when one is treated with politeness and kindness in buses, trains, trams, subways, ferries, stores, shops, and streets.   JOHN COWPER POWYS

The cobra will bite you whether you call it cobra or Mr. Cobra.

INDIAN PROVERB

There can be no defence like elaborate courtesy.   E. V. LUCAS

CREATIVITY

The thing that makes a creative person is to be creative and that is all there is to it.   EDWARD ALBEE

The very essence of the creative is its novelty, and hence we have no standard by which to judge it.   CARL R. ROGERS

The deepest experience of the creator is feminine, for it is the experience of receiving and bearing.   RAINER MARIA RILKE

Our current obsession with creativity is the result of our continued striving for immortality in an era when most people no longer believe in an afterlife.   ARIANNA STASSINOPOULOS

Joy is but the sign that creative emotion is fulfilling its purpose.

CHARLES DU BOS

Creativity requires the freedom to consider "unthinkable" alternatives, to doubt the worth of cherished practices.   JOHN W. GARDNER

I'm nobody's steady date. I can always be distracted by love, but eventually I get horny for my creativity.   GILDA RADNER

When the creative urge seizes one—at least, such is my experience— one becomes creative in all directions at once.   HENRY MILLER

Every individual who is not creative has a negative, narrow exclusive taste and succeeds in depriving creative being of its energy and life.   GOETHE

CRIME

Unless we have a safe society, we are not going to have a free society.   ROBERT C. BYRD

The way to reduce crime is to convince the criminal that, upon the commission of a crime, he will be speedily apprehended, convicted, and punished.   THOMAS A. FLANNERY

We don't give our criminals much punishment, but we sure give 'em plenty of publicity.   WILL ROGERS

If the desire to kill and the opportunity to kill came always together, who would escape hanging?   MARK TWAIN

To spare the ravening leopard is an act of injustice to the sheep.   PERSIAN PROVERB

Eight out of ten guys who hit you over the head on the streets have learned their trade in prison.   MELVIN BELLI

No radical change on the plane of history is possible without crime.   COUNT HERMANN KEYSERLING

We cannot control crime without controlling the random and wanton distribution of guns.   LYNDON B. JOHNSON

It is well-nigh obvious that those who are in favor of the death penalty have more affinities with murderers than those who oppose it.   REMY DE GOURMONT

A criminal becomes a popular figure because he unburdens in no small degree the consciences of his fellow man, for now they know once more where evil is to be found.   CARL G. JUNG

CRITICISM

I like criticism when it is constructive; then it helps me. But when someone is critical just to be mean or tear something down, I must go away from that person. It depresses me.   SOPHIA LOREN

We must have passed through life unobservantly, if we have never perceived that a man is very much himself what he thinks of others.   FREDERICK W. FABER

It is salutary to train oneself to be no more affected by censure than by praise.   W. SOMERSET MAUGHAM

It is uncommon hard to annihilate a man with words—although it is often undertook.   JOSH BILLINGS

He has the right to criticize who has the heart to help.   ABRAHAM LINCOLN

To avoid criticism, do nothing, say nothing, be nothing.   ELBERT HUBBARD

Abuse, hearty abuse, is a tonic to all save men of indifferent health.   NORMAN DOUGLAS

You will find that out of a dozen people who like something in public improvements one will write a letter about it or say something about it. If they don't like something, eleven out of twelve will tell you that. That seems to be human nature.   ROBERT MOSES

Living in the public eye accustoms one to accept criticism. One learns gradually to take it objectively and to try to think of it as directed at somebody else and evaluate whether it is just or unjust.   ELEANOR ROOSEVELT

CRITICISM, LITERARY

The besetting weakness of criticism, when faced with a new writer, is to define his work too narrowly, and then to keep applying that definition like a label.   F. O. MATTHIESSEN

Critics have a right to be modest and a duty to be vain.   KARL KRAUS

I can imagine nothing more distressing to a critic than to have a writer see accurately into his own work.   NORMAN MAILER

O ye critics, will nothing melt ye?   SIR WALTER SCOTT

The lovely thing about critics is when they have a big target, they belt 'em. Because it's more fun.   HAROLD ROBBINS

A critic has no right to the narrowness which is the frequent prerogative of the creative artist. He has to have a wide outlook or he has not anything at all.   E. M. FORSTER

One does not value even a dog if he wags his tail for everybody, and it is the same way with a critic.   FRANK MOORE COLBY

Criticism is a profession by which men grow formidable and important at very small expense.   SAMUEL JOHNSON

DAY

They deem me mad because I will not sell my days for gold; and I deem them mad because they think my days have a price.
KAHLIL GIBRAN

Each day, and the living of it, has to be a conscious creation in which discipline and order are relieved with some play and some pure foolishness.   MAY SARTON

Men can bear all things except good days.   DUTCH PROVERB

The day is of infinite length for him who knows how to appreciate and use it.   GOETHE

To sensible men, every day is a day of reckoning. JOHN W. GARDNER

DEATH

Death is for many of us the gate of hell; but we are inside on the way out, not outside on the way in.   GEORGE BERNARD SHAW

We understand death for the first time when he puts his hand upon one whom we love.   MADAME DE STAEL

He said he was dying of fast women, slow horses, crooked cards, and straight whiskey.   KENNETH REXROTH,
referring to his father

There is no death. Only a change of worlds.   CHIEF SEATTLE,
of the Dwamish tribe

If the general had known how big a funeral he was going to have, he would have died years ago.   ABRAHAM LINCOLN

It costs a lot of money to die comfortably.   SAMUEL BUTLER

I want a priest, a rabbi, and a Protestant clergyman. I want to hedge my bets.   WILSON MIZNER

What is the world to a man when his wife is a widow.

IRISH PROVERB

DECISION

In the important decisions of personal life, we should be governed, I think, by the deep inner needs of our nature.   SIGMUND FREUD

Now who is to decide between "let it be" and "force it"?

KATHERINE MANSFIELD

It does not take much strength to do things, but it requires great strength to decide on what to do.   ELBERT HUBBARD

If we are ever in doubt about what to do, it is a good rule to ask ourselves what we shall wish on the morrow that we had done.

SIR JOHN LUBBOCK

When once I have made my decision, I go straight to my end, and sweep aside everything with my red cassock.   CARDINAL RICHELIEU

A weak man has doubts before a decision; a strong man has them afterwards.   KARL KRAUS

DEMOCRACY

The test of democracy is freedom of criticism.   DAVID BEN-GURION

It is a constant hazard of democracy that the loudest and most determined group is often that which holds the most extreme and reactionary views.   PIERRE ELLIOTT TRUDEAU

Democracy is like a raft: It won't sink, but you will always have your feet wet.   RUSSELL B. LONG

If the equality of individuals and the dignity of man be myths, they are myths to which the republic is committed.

HOWARD MUMFORD JONES

Whatever may be truly said about the good sense of a democracy during a great crisis, at ordinary times it does not bring the best men to the top.   WILLIAM R. INGE

Man's capacity for justice makes democracy possible; but man's inclination to injustice makes democracy necessary.

REINHOLD NIEBUHR

DESIRE

If men could regard the events of their own lives with more open minds, they would frequently discover that they did not really desire the things they failed to obtain.   ANDRÉ MAUROIS

Have the courage of your desire.   GEORGE GISSING

If you don't get everything you want, think of the things you don't get that you don't want.   OSCAR WILDE

Believe me, for certain men at least, not taking what one doesn't desire is the hardest thing in the world.   ALBERT CAMUS

One half of knowing what you want is knowing what you must give up before you get it.   SIDNEY HOWARD

Many people think they want things, but they don't really have the strength, the discipline. They are weak. I believe that you get what you want if you want it badly enough.   SOPHIA LOREN

DEVIL

The Devil is most devilish when respectable.

ELIZABETH BARRETT BROWNING

If Hitler invaded Hell I would make at least favorable reference to the Devil in the House of Commons.   SIR WINSTON CHURCHILL

All religions issue bibles against him, and say most injurious things about him, but we never hear *his* side.   MARK TWAIN

In all systems of theology the devil figures as a male person. . . . Yes, it is the women who keep the churches going.   DON MARQUIS

The Devil, having nothing else to do,
Went off to tempt My Lady Poltagrue.
My Lady, tempted by a private whim,
To his extreme annoyance, tempted him.
                                    HILAIRE BELLOC,
                          "Our Lady Poltagrue, A Public Peril"

DIET

If you want to feel important, go on a diet.   JOEY ADAMS

I feel about diets the way I feel about airplanes. They're wonderful things for other people to go on.   JEAN KERR

Thinness is more naked, more indecent, than corpulence.
                                    CHARLES BAUDELAIRE

Dietitians are the worst enemy of the great cuisine. It is impossible to have low calories in excellent food.   LOUIS VAUDABLE

He who takes medicine and neglects to diet wastes the skill of his doctors.   CHINESE PROVERB

The one way to get thin is to reestablish a purpose in life.
                                    CYRIL CONNOLLY

DIFFICULTY

Not everything that is more difficult is more meritorious.
                                    SAINT THOMAS AQUINAS

To behold difficult objects lightly handled gives us the impression of the impossible.   GOETHE

The greater the difficulty the more glory in surmounting it.
                                    EPICURUS

The habits of a vigorous mind are formed in contending with difficulties . . . great necessities call out great virtues.   ABIGAIL ADAMS

The course of true anything never does run smooth.
                                    SAMUEL BUTLER

In difficulty you understand your friends.   CHINESE PROVERB

DIPLOMACY

A diplomat's life is made up of three ingredients: Protocol, Geritol, and alcohol.   ADLAI E. STEVENSON

Let us never negotiate out of fear. But let us never fear to negotiate.   JOHN F. KENNEDY

Diplomacy: The business of handling a porcupine without disturbing the quills.   ANONYMOUS

Diplomacy: The art of saying "nice doggie" until you can find a rock.   WYNN CATLIN

Once the Xerox copier was invented, private diplomacy died. There's no such thing as secrecy. It's just a question of whether it's leaked or revealed openly.   ANDREW YOUNG

Conferences at the top level are always courteous. Name-calling is left to the foreign ministers.   W. AVERELL HARRIMAN

Diplomats are useful only in fair weather. As soon as it rains they drown in every drop.   CHARLES DE GAULLE

DIVORCE

I believe in divorce because again and again we must have in marriage, as in every other experience of life, a decent corrective of mistake and tragedy.   JOHN HAYNES HOLMES

Weddings are always the same, but no divorces are alike.
    WILL ROGERS

Divorce is not the enemy of marriage, it is its ally.
    DR. JOSEPH COLLINS

Alimony is like buying oats for a dead horse. ARTHUR ("BUGS") BAER

The desire for divorce is the only important factor. The reasons do not matter.   HEYWOOD HALE BROUN

Judges, as a class, display, in the matter of arranging alimony, that reckless generosity which is found only in men who are giving away somebody else's cash.   P. G. WODEHOUSE

DOCTOR

One of the first duties of the physician is to educate the masses not to take medicine.   SIR WILLIAM OSLER

No physician is really good before he has killed one or two patients.
                    HINDU PROVERB

Ever since I was a little girl I poured all the medicine doctors ever gave me down the drain and planted their pills in my flower pots.
                    MRS. EDMONA COLLINS,
                    Linesville, Pennsylvania,
                    on her hundredth birthday.

Doctors think a lot of patients are cured who have simply quit in disgust.   DON HEROLD

I wonder why you can always read a doctor's bill and you can never read his prescription.   FINLEY PETER DUNNE

I would like to see the day when somebody would be appointed surgeon somewhere who had no hands, for the operative part is the least part of the work.   DR. HARVEY CUSHING

Heaven defend me from a busy doctor.   WELSH PROVERB

Some doctors make the same mistakes for twenty years and call it clinical experience.   DR. NOAH D. FABRICANT

Being a physican certainly doesn't make one immune to human suffering, nor should it, but one does become less vulnerable if there is happiness in one's own life.   SIGMUND FREUD

It seems to me that a doctor's is the most perfect of all lives; it satisfies the craving to know, and also the craving to serve.
                    OLIVE SCHREINER

The trouble with doctors, I find, is that they seldom admit that anything stumps them.   GEORGE JEAN NATHAN

DOG

I had only one friend, my dog. My wife was mad at me, and I told her a man ought to have at least two friends. She agreed—and bought me another dog.   PEPPER RODGERS,
                    UCLA coach

People who do not clean up after their dogs obviously have yet to complete their own toilet training.   BRENDAN FRANCIS

The great pleasure of a dog is that you may make a fool out of yourself with him and not only will he not scold you, but he will make a fool of himself too.   SAMUEL BUTLER

Our dogs will love and admire the meanest of us, and feed our colossal vanity with their uncritical homage.   AGNES REPPLIER

A dog with money is addressed as "Mr. Dog."   SPANISH PROVERB

If dogs could talk, perhaps we would find it as hard to get along with them as we do with people.   KAREL ČAPEK

The dog is a yes-animal, very popular with people who can't afford to keep a yes-man.   ROBERTSON DAVIES

Big dogs like to sleep peacefully before fires; the little yap-yaps, who are always nipping away at people's ankles, start trouble.

GEORGE SANDERS

Wanted: A dog that neither barks nor bites, eats broken glass and shits diamonds.   GOETHE

DOING

Our dignity is not in what we do, but what we understand. The whole world is doing things.   GEORGE SANTAYANA

Generally speaking anybody is more interesting doing nothing than doing anything.   GERTRUDE STEIN

The shortest answer is doing.   ENGLISH PROVERB

What we love to do we find time to do.   JOHN LANCASTER SPALDING

Now the only decent way to get something done is to get it done by somebody who quite likes doing it.   D. H. LAWRENCE

DOUBT

If you doubt yourself, then indeed you stand on shaky ground.

HENRIK IBSEN

I respect faith, but doubt is what gets you an education.

WILSON MIZNER

No man likes to have his intelligence or good faith questioned, especially if he has doubts about it himself.   HENRY ADAMS

Doubt of any kind cannot be resolved except by action.

THOMAS CARLYLE

The trouble with the world is that the stupid are cocksure and the intelligent full of doubt.   BERTRAND RUSSELL

DREAM

A dream grants what one covets when awake.   GERMAN PROVERB

I should have lost many a good hit, had I not set down at once things that occurred to me in my dreams.   SIR WALTER SCOTT

Recall the old story of the rather refined young man who preferred sex dreams to visiting brothels because he met a much nicer type of girl that way.   VIVIAN MERCER

My young men never work. Men who work cannot dream; and wisdom comes to us in dreams.   CHIEF SMOHALL,
of the Nez Percé

Dreaming permits each and every one of us to be quietly and safely insane every night of our lives.   DR. WILLIAM DEMENT

DRINKING

A man takes a drink, the drink takes another, and the drink takes the man.   SINCLAIR LEWIS

A soft drink turneth away company.   OLIVER HERFORD

In a world where there is a law against people ever showing their emotions, or ever releasing themselves from the grayness of their days, a drink is not a social tool. It is a thing you need in order to live.   JIMMY BRESLIN

One reason I don't drink is that I want to know when I am having a good time.   LADY ASTOR

They speak of my drinking, but never think of my thirst.

SCOTTISH PROVERB

For a bad hangover take the juice of two quarts of whisky.

EDDIE CONDON

DRUGS

Drugs are marvelous if you want to escape, but reality is so rich, why escape? GERALDINE CHAPLIN

Anything that can be done chemically can be done in other ways— that is, if we have sufficient knowledge of the processes involved.

WILLIAM BURROUGHS

If you haven't paid the real wages of love or courage or abstention or discipline or sacrifice or wit in the eye of danger, then taking a psychedelic drug is living the life of a parasite; it's drawing on sweets you have not earned. NORMAN MAILER

DUTY

When a stupid man is doing something he is ashamed of, he always declares that it is his duty. GEORGE BERNARD SHAW

Only he who is uncompromising as to his rights maintains the sense of duty. ALBERT CAMUS

We need to restore the full meaning of that old word, duty. It is the other side of rights. PEARL BUCK

Duty does not have to be dull. Love can make it beautiful and fill it with life. THOMAS MERTON

Every duty which is bidden to wait returns with seven fresh duties at its back. CHARLES KINGSLEY

Duty is the sublimest word in the language; you can never do more than your duty; you should never wish to do less. ROBERT E. LEE

Every duty we omit obscures some truth we should have known.

JOHN RUSKIN

Duty is what one expects from others. OSCAR WILDE

EARTH

How can the spirit of the earth like the white man? . . . Everywhere the white man has touched it, it is sore.

AN OLD WINTU INDIAN WOMAN

What you cannot find on earth is not worth seeking.

NORMAN DOUGLAS

Be the earth great or small, what does that matter to mankind? It is always great enough as long as it gives us a stage for suffering and for love.   ANATOLE FRANCE

The earth is a Paradise, the only one we will ever know. We will realize it the moment we open our eyes. We don't have to make it a Paradise—it *is* one. We have only to make ourselves fit to inhabit it.

HENRY MILLER

EDITORS AND EDITING

Editing is the same thing as quarreling with writers—same thing exactly.   HAROLD ROSS

Editors are extremely fallible people, all of them. Don't put too much trust in them.   MAXWELL PERKINS

An editor is a man who knows what he wants, but doesn't know what it is.   WALTER DAVENPORT

No author dislikes to be edited as much as he dislikes not to be published.   RUSSELL LYNES

The first obligation of one who lives by writing is to write what editors will buy.   CHRISTOPHER MORLEY

The job of editor in a publishing house is the dullest, hardest, most exciting, exasperating, and rewarding of perhaps any job in the world.   JOHN HALL WHEELOCK

EDUCATION

Everything must be made as simple as possible but not one bit simpler.   ALBERT EINSTEIN

One of the unfortunate things about our education system is that we do not teach students how to avail themselves of their subconscious capabilities.   BILL LEAR

It doesn't make much difference what you study, as long as you don't like it.   FINLEY PETER DUNNE

We are now at the point where we must educate people in what nobody knew yesterday, and prepare in our schools for what no one knows yet but what some people must know tomorrow.

MARGARET MEAD

Education is the ability to listen to almost anything without losing your temper or your self-confidence.   ROBERT FROST

The school is the last expenditure upon which America should be willing to economize.   FRANKLIN D. ROOSEVELT

His studies were pursued but never effectually overtaken.

H. G. WELLS

I am entirely certain that twenty years from now we will look back at education as it is practiced in most schools today and wonder that we could have tolerated anything so primitive.

JOHN W. GARDNER

A young man who is not a radical about something is a pretty poor risk for education.   JACQUES BARZUN

Does college pay? They do if you are a good open-field runner.

WILL ROGERS

What is learned in high school, or for that matter anywhere at all, depends far less on what is taught than on what one actually experiences in the place.   EDGAR Z. FRIEDENBERG

A wise system of education will at least teach us how little man yet knows, how much he has still to learn.   SIR JOHN LUBBOCK

EFFORT

God gives no linen, but flax to spin.   GERMAN PROVERB

We strain hardest for things which are almost but not quite within our reach.   FREDERICK W. FABER

Nothing got without pains but an ill name and long nails.

SCOTTISH PROVERB

If experience went for anything, we should all come to a standstill; for there is nothing so discouraging as effort.

CHARLES DUDLEY WARNER

The trite objects of human efforts—possessions, outward success, luxury—have always seemed to me contemptible.   ALBERT EINSTEIN

EGOTISM

In all that surrounds him the egotist sees only the frame of his own portrait.   J. PETIT-SENN

Nothing is so interesting as egotism when a man has an ego.

FRANK HARRIS

An egotist is a man who thinks that a woman will marry him for himself alone.   ANONYMOUS

The average man is not half enough of an egotist. If egotism means a terrific interest in one's self, egotism is absolutely essential to efficient living.   ARNOLD BENNETT

What's wrong with this egotism? If a man doesn't delight in himself and the force in him and feel that he and it are wonders, how is all life to become important to him?   SHERWOOD ANDERSON

Some people, when they hear an echo, think they originated the sound.   ERNEST HEMINGWAY

You will commonly find most egotism in reserved people.

JOSEPH FARRELL

ELOQUENCE

The finest eloquence is that which gets things done.

DAVID LLOYD GEORGE

Eloquence is the power to translate a truth into language perfectly intelligible to the person to whom you speak.

RALPH WALDO EMERSON

Eloquence is vehement simplicity.   RICHARD CECIL

True eloquence foregoes eloquence.   ANDRÉ GIDE

To speak and to speak well are two things. A fool may talk, but a wise man speaks.   BEN JONSON

He need not search his pockets for words.   RUSSIAN PROVERB

Eloquence is in the assembly, not merely in the speaker.
                                                    WILLIAM PITT

EMOTION

Cherish your own emotions and never undervalue them.
                                                    ROBERT HENRI

Many a man is afraid of expressing honest emotion because the word "sentimental" frightens him.   HILAIRE BELLOC

To give vent now and then to his feelings, whether of pleasure or discontent, is a great ease to a man's heart. FRANCESCO GUICCIARDINI

Seeing's believing, but feeling is God's own truth.   IRISH PROVERB

It is always one of the tragedies of any relationship, even between people sensitive to each other's moods, that the moments of emotion so rarely coincide.   NAN FAIRBROTHER

My emotions flowered in me like a divine revelation.   ANDRÉ GIDE

It is terribly amusing how many different climates of feeling one can go through in one day.   ANNE MORROW LINDBERGH

ENCOURAGEMENT

Encouragement after censure is as the sun after a shower.   GOETHE

All we can ever do in the way of good to people is to encourage them to do good to themselves.   RANDOLPH BOURNE

There is nothing better than the encouragement of a good friend.
                                        KATHARINE BUTLER HATHAWAY

Providence seldom vouchsafes to mortals any more than just that degree of encouragement which suffices to keep them at a reasonably full exertion of their powers.   NATHANIEL HAWTHORNE

ENDURANCE

Nothing great was ever done without much enduring.

SAINT CATHERINE OF SIENA

Enjoy when you can, and endure when you must.   GOETHE

A man can bear more than ten oxen can pull.   YIDDISH PROVERB

He conquers who endures.   PERSIUS

One may go a long way after one is tired.   FRENCH PROVERB

ENEMY

Instead of loving your enemies, treat your friends a little better.

E. W. HOWE

If you have no enemies, you are apt to be in the same predicament in regard to friends.   ELBERT HUBBARD

Use your enemy's hand to catch a snake.   PERSIAN PROVERB

Love your enemies. It makes them so damned mad.   P. D. EAST

I wish my deadly foe no worse than want of friends and an empty purse.   NICHOLAS BRETON

Our friends may be the undoing of us; in the end it is our enemies who save us.   HAVELOCK ELLIS

Often we attack and make ourselves enemies, to conceal that we are vulnerable.   FRIEDRICH NIETZSCHE

ENGLAND AND THE ENGLISH

If the British can survive their meals, they can survive anything.

GEORGE BERNARD SHAW

England is my wife—America, my mistress. It is very good sometimes to get away from one's wife.   SIR CEDRIC HARDWICKE

In order to appreciate England one has to have a certain contempt for logic.   LIN YUTANG

That is why I love England. It is so little, and so full, and so old.

ROBERT SPEAIGHT

And you do admire a little overmuch English detachment. It often is mere indifference and lack of life.   D. H. LAWRENCE

England is not . . . the best possible world but it is the best actual country, and a great rest after America.   GEORGE SANTAYANA

Except when it comes to bravery, we are a nation of mice. We dress and behave with timid circumspection.   EDITH SITWELL

Three things to beware of: the hoof of a horse, the horn of a bull, and the smile of an Englishman.   SEUMAS MAC MANUS

You English are hard. You do not know when you are beaten.

CAPT. HANS LANGSDORFF,
commander of the Graf Spee

The whole strength of England lies in the fact that the enormous majority of the English people are snobs.   GEORGE BERNARD SHAW

I know better than to argue when the English talk about their duty.   RUDYARD KIPLING

ENTHUSIASM

A man can succeed at almost anything for which he has unlimited enthusiasm.   CHARLES SCHWAB

The enthusiastic, to those who are not, are always something of a trial.   ALBAN GOODIER

The world belongs to the enthusiast who keeps cool.

WILLIAM MC FEE

No one, looking back, ever really regrets one of his young enthusiasms. It is the enthusiasms we did not have that we regret.

J. W. MACKAIL

Like simplicity and candor, and other much-commended qualities, enthusiasm is charming until we meet it face to face, and cannot escape from its charm.   AGNES REPPLIER

Every great and commanding moment in the annals of the world is the triumph of some enthusiasm.   RALPH WALDO EMERSON

Enthusiasm finds the opportunities, and energy makes the most of them.   HENRY S. HASKINS

ENVY

Envy is thin because it bites but never eats.   SPANISH PROVERB

The envious man does not die only once but as many times as the person he envies lives to hear the voice of praise. BALTASAR GRACIAN

Beggars do not envy millionaires, though of course they will envy other beggars who are more successful.   BERTRAND RUSSELL

It is a sickening thing to think how many angry and evil passions the mere name of admitted excellence brings into full activity.

SIR WALTER SCOTT

I doubt whether Saint Simeon Stylites would have been wholly pleased if he had learned of some other saint who had stood even longer on an even narrower pillar.   BERTRAND RUSSELL

It is hard to endure envy, but much harder to have nothing worth envying.   LATIN PROVERB

EQUALITY

Before God and the bus driver we are all equal.   GERMAN PROVERB

We will have equality when a female schlemiel moves ahead as fast as a male schlemiel.   ESTELLE RAMEY

We are not created equal, and our differences are often greater than our similarities.   CARLTON FREDERICKS

If all were equal, if all were rich, and if all were at table who would lay the cloth?   GERMAN PROVERB

When there were no human rights, the exceptional individual had them. That was inhuman. Then equality was created by taking the human rights away from the exceptional individual.   KARL KRAUS

Of equality—As if it harm'd me, giving others the same chances and rights as myself—As if it were not indispensable to my own rights that others possess the same.   WALT WHITMAN

After death all men smell alike.   ITALIAN PROVERB

EVIL

Every evil is some good spelt backwards, and in it the wise know how to read Wisdom. COVENTRY PATMORE

The seduction of evil is precisely in that it involves us in trying to eliminate it. THADDEUS GOLAS

Evil is a hill; each one gets on his own and speaks about someone else's. AFRICAN PROVERB

Nonresistance to evil which takes the form of paying no attention to it is a way of promoting it. JOHN DEWEY

The hardest fact in the world to accept is the inevitable mixture of evil with good in all things. AUSTIN O'MALLEY

It is tempting to deny the existence of evil since denying it obviates the need to fight it. ALEXIS CARREL

What we think the greatest evils in our minute lives often bring to us the greatest blessings. It may be so with nations.
JOHN JAY CHAPMAN

Everything evil is revenge. OTTO WEININGER

EXCELLENCE

If you wish to make people stare by doing better than others, why, make them stare till they stare their eyes out. SAMUEL JOHNSON

You will always do much, if you accomplish perfectly what you do.
A. D. SERTILLANGES

Everything superlatively good has always been quantitatively small, and scarce. BALTASAR GRACIAN

When a thing is thoroughly well done it often has the air of being a miracle. ARNOLD BENNETT

Hit the ball over the fence and you can take your time going around the bases. JOHN W. RAPER

One of the rarest things that a man ever does is to do the best he can. JOSH BILLINGS

EXERCISE

Faddists are continually proclaiming the value of exercise; four out of five people are more in need of rest than exercise.

DR. LOGAN CLENDENING

Vanity is at the bottom of much of the exercise indulged in by men after their youth is gone; the question of health is of second consideration.   GEORGE JEAN NATHAN

Those who do not find time for exercise will have to find time for illness.   OLD PROVERB

Any workout which does not involve a certain minimum of danger or responsibility does not improve the body—it just wears it out.

NORMAN MAILER

EXPECTATION

It is a common observation that those who dwell continually upon their expectations are apt to become oblivious to the requirements of their actual situation.   CHARLES SANDERS PEIRCE

What a wonderful world this would be if we all did as well today as we expect to do tomorrow.   ANONYMOUS

Nothing is so good as it seems beforehand.   GEORGE ELIOT

Men have a trick of coming up to what is expected of them, good or bad.   JACOB RIIS

Men expect too much, do too little.   ALLEN TATE

Our expectation of what the human animal can learn, can do, can be, remains remarkably low and timorous.   GEORGE B. LEONARD

As a man gets wiser, he expects less, and probably gets more than he expects.   JOSEPH FARRELL

EXPERIENCE

Experience is a name everyone gives to their mistakes. OSCAR WILDE

Experience should teach us that it is always the unexpected that does occur.   ELEANOR ROOSEVELT

What a strange narrowness of mind now is that, to think the things we have not known are better than the things we have known.

SAMUEL JOHNSON

Experience is not what happens to you; it is what you do with what happens to you.   ALDOUS HUXLEY

Experience makes more timid men than it does wise ones.

JOSH BILLINGS

Experience does not teach us that every enthusiasm is absurd. From it we learn simply to wait for results, not from high-sounding words, but from hard work and great courage.   ANDRÉ MAUROIS

Some people have had nothing else but experience.   DON HEROLD

EXPLANATION

When you don't know much about a subject you are explaining, compliment the person you are explaining to on knowing all about it and he will think that you do, too.   DON MARQUIS

"Shut up!" he explained.   RING LARDNER

I have always been willing to make an explanation, but never an excuse, for doing anything I considered proper.

ELEANOR ROOSEVELT

I fear explanations explanatory of things explained.

ABRAHAM LINCOLN

I am the master of everything I can explain.   THEODOR HAECKER

You should avoid making yourself too clear even in your explanations.   BALTASAR GRACIAN

No explanation ever explains the necessity of making one.

ELBERT HUBBARD

FACE

As they grow older, human beings acquire the faces they deserve.

OWEN D. YOUNG

Plainness has its peculiar temptations quite as much as beauty.

GEORGE ELIOT

Somehow, people with nice faces inspire me with more confidence than those who I am assured have beautiful minds. One can see their faces—that makes so much difference.   E. F. BENSON

Trust not too much to an enchanting face.   VIRGIL

The Methodists have acquired a face; the Quakers, a face; the nuns, a face.   RALPH WALDO EMERSON

I never forget a face, but in your case I'll make an exception.
                    GROUCHO MARX

Her face was her chaperone.   RUPERT HUGHES

It is the common wonder of all men, how among so many millions of faces there should be none alike.   SIR THOMAS BROWNE

FACT

There is no sadder sight in the world than to see a beautiful theory killed by a brutal fact.   THOMAS HENRY HUXLEY

I have steadily endeavoured to keep my mind free so as to give up any hypothesis, however much beloved . . . as soon as facts are shown to be opposed to it.   CHARLES DARWIN

Facts do not cease to exist just because they are ignored.
                    ALDOUS HUXLEY

One of the most untruthful things possible, you know, is a collection of facts, because they can be made to appear so many different ways.   DR. KARL A. MENNINGER

Get your facts first, and then you can distort them as much as you please.   MARK TWAIN

FAILURE

Half the failures in life arise from pulling in one's horse as he is leaping.   J. C. and A. W. HARE

I never blame failures—there are too many complicated situations in life, but I am absolutely merciless toward lack of effort.
                    F. SCOTT FITZGERALD

Notice the difference between what happens when a man says to himself, "I have failed three times," and what happens when he says, "I am a failure."   S. I. HAYAKAWA

The probability that we shall fail in the struggle should not deter us from the support of a cause we believe to be just.

ABRAHAM LINCOLN

The men who try to do something and fail are infinitely better than those who try to do nothing and succeed.   LLOYD JONES

One of the reasons mature people stop learning is that they become less and less willing to risk failure.   JOHN W. GARDNER

I don't know the key to success, but the key to failure is trying to please everybody.   BILL COSBY

FAITH

Faith which does not doubt is a dead faith.   MIGUEL DE UNAMUNO

I admire the serene assurance of those who have religious faith. It is wonderful to observe the calm confidence of a Christian with four aces.   MARK TWAIN

Faith is the bird that feels the light when the dawn is still dark.

RABINDRANATH TAGORE

It is a fact of human nature that men can live and die by the help of a sort of faith that goes without a single dogma or definition.

WILLIAM JAMES

Faith is the sturdiest, the most manly of the virtues. . . . It is the virtue of the storm, just as happiness is the virtue of the sunshine.

RUTH BENEDICT

FAME

If you acquire fame, people begin putting you outside themselves. You are something special. Who wants to be that?

SHERWOOD ANDERSON

Man dreads fame as a pig dreads fat.   ORIENTAL PROVERB

Martyrdom is the only way in which a man can become famous
without ability.   GEORGE BERNARD SHAW

A celebrity is one who is known to many persons he is glad he
doesn't know.   H. L. MENCKEN

Men often mistake notoriety for fame, and would rather be remembered for their vices and follies than not to be noticed at all.
                                          HARRY S. TRUMAN

A man comes to be famous because he has the matter for fame
within him. To seek for, to hunt after fame, is a vain endeavor.
                                                  GOETHE

A man who is much talked about is always very attractive.
                                             OSCAR WILDE

FAMILY

The horizons of women all over the world are widening from home
to humanity—from our private families to the family of man.
                                        LADY BIRD JOHNSON

Families, I hate you! Shut-in living, closed doors, jealous protectors
of happiness.   ANDRÉ GIDE

There's plenty of peace in any home where the family don't make
the mistake of trying to get together.   KIN HUBBARD

In every dispute between parent and child, both cannot be right,
but they may be, and usually are, both wrong. It is this situation
which gives family life its peculiar hysterical charm.
                                          ISAAC ROSENFELD

It is easier to rule a kingdom than to regulate a family.
                                          JAPANESE PROVERB

The families of one's friends are always a disappointment.
                                           NORMAN DOUGLAS

There are several ways in which to apportion the family income,
all of them unsatisfactory.   ROBERT BENCHLEY

I, who have no sisters or brothers, look with some degree of innocent envy on those who may be said to be born to friends.
                                            JAMES BOSWELL

FARM

If God gave me the choice of the whole planet or my little farm, I should certainly take my farm.   RALPH WALDO EMERSON

One good thing about living on a farm is that you can fight with your wife without being heard.   KIN HUBBARD

Did anybody ever buy a farm without seeing some reason for adding a little more to it? . . . A hundred acres are never content without fifty more.   HENRY WARD BEECHER

I am impressed by certain things about farmers. One of them is their destructiveness. One of them is their total lack of the appreciation of the beautiful—in the main. There are exceptions.
    DR. KARL A. MENNINGER

FASHION

The truly fashionable are beyond fashion.   CECIL BEATON

It [bralessness] is not a very uplifting subject. Personally, I'm a firm believer in not tipping one's hand, or, in this case, other portions of one's anatomy. I've been getting by for years on what I didn't show the boys.   MAE WEST

If I were a woman I wouldn't wear an obviously unbecoming hat just because it was the latest decree of fashion. WILLIAM ROSE BENÉT

Today, someone can put on a T-shirt and be extremely elegant, because there's elegance in that human being.   RUDI GERNREICH

Fashion is a tool . . . to compete in life outside the home. People like you better, without knowing why, because people always react well to a person they like the looks of.   MARY QUANT

Blue jeans? They should be worn by farm girls milking cows!
    YVES SAINT LAURENT

Just around the corner in every woman's mind—is a lovely dress, a wonderful suit, or entire costume which will make an enchanting new creature of her.   WILHELA CUSHMAN

No matter how low their necks are cut, or how short their skirts get, we'll always have to take chances on their real dispositions.
    KIN HUBBARD

I base most of my fashion taste on what doesn't itch. GILDA RADNER

My idea of chic is that everyone in the world would have the same dress and the chicest woman would be whoever could do the best thing with it.   NORMAN NORELL

He who goes against the fashion is himself its slave.

LOGAN PEARSALL SMITH

I don't know what it is. I have girls on my staff who haven't the brains of a button, but send them out in the market and they will come back with the best hat or shoes or dress of the season.

DIANA VREELAND

The woman who dresses well draws her husband from another woman's door.   SPANISH PROVERB

FATE

So, after all, we are but puppets, creatures of our fate, not commanding it but being molded by it.   ELEANOR ROOSEVELT

When its time has arrived, the prey comes to the hunter.

PERSIAN PROVERB

The day of fate tarries and not till it arrives will the authentic direction be spoken. Meantime suspense.   JOHN DEWEY

I was thinking of my patients, and how the worst moment for them was when they discovered they were masters of their own fate. It was not a matter of bad or good luck. When they could no longer blame fate, they were in despair.   ANAÏS NIN

There's much to be said for challenging fate instead of ducking behind it.   DIANA TRILLING

Fate determines many things, no matter how we struggle.

OTTO WEININGER

FATHER

The most important thing a father can do for his children is to love their mother.   REV. THEODORE HESBURGH

Two little girls, on their way home from Sunday school, were solemnly discussing the lesson. "Do you believe there is a devil?" asked one. "No," said the other promptly. "It's like Santa Claus: it's your father."   LADIES' HOME JOURNAL

Perhaps host and guest is really the happiest relation for father and son.   EVELYN WAUGH

Children suck the mother when they are young and the father when they are old.   ENGLISH PROVERB

When I was a kid, I used to imagine animals running under my bed. I told my dad, and he solved the problem quickly. He cut the legs off the bed.   LOU BROCK

If you've never seen a real, fully developed look of disgust, just tell your son how you conducted yourself when you were a boy.

KIN HUBBARD

Don't be a lion in your house.   CZECH PROVERB

Once an angry man dragged his father along the ground through his own orchard. "Stop!" cried the groaning old man at last, "Stop! I did not drag my father beyond this tree." GERTRUDE STEIN

My daddy doesn't work, he just goes to the office; but sometimes he does errands on the way home.   ANONYMOUS LITTLE GIRL

I could not point to any need in childhood as strong as that for a father's protection.   SIGMUND FREUD

If a man smiles at home somebody is sure to ask him for money.

WILLIAM C. FEATHER

There must always be a struggle between a father and a son, while one aims at power the other at independence.   SAMUEL JOHNSON

Father and son are natural enemies and each is happier and more secure in keeping it that way.   JOHN STEINBECK

FAULT

Unless I accept my faults I will most certainly doubt my virtues.

HUGH PRATHER

Think of your faults the first part of the night when you are awake, and the faults of others the latter part of the night when you are asleep.   CHINESE PROVERB

A diamond with a flaw is better than a common stone that is perfect.   CHINESE PROVERB

People who have no faults are terrible; there is no way of taking advantage of them.   ANATOLE FRANCE

Happy people rarely correct their faults.   LA ROCHEFOUCAULD

The imperfections of a man, his frailties, his faults, are just as important as his virtues. You can't separate them. They're wedded.
                                                       HENRY MILLER

There are no faults in a thing we want badly.   ARAB PROVERB

'Tis a great confidence in a friend to tell him your faults; greater to tell him his.   BENJAMIN FRANKLIN

An infatuated young man sought counsel at the bazaar of an ancient and prayed the ancient to tell him how he might learn of his fair lady's faults. "Go forth among her women friends," spake the venerable one, "and praise her in their hearing."
                                                 GEORGE JEAN NATHAN

Failings I am always rather rejoiced to find in a man than sorry for; they bring us to a level.   JOHN KEATS

He is great whose faults can be numbered.   HEBREW PROVERB

FEAR

Fear is static that prevents me from hearing my intuition.
                                                       HUGH PRATHER

The first and great commandment is, don't let them scare you.
                                                       ELMER DAVIS

All the passions seek whatever nourishes them: fear loves the idea of danger.   JOSEPH JOUBERT

What you are afraid of overtakes you.   ESTONIAN PROVERB

Perhaps the most important thing we can undertake toward the

reduction of fear is to make it easier for people to accept themselves; to like themselves.   BONARO OVERSTREET

Many of our fears are tissue-paper-thin, and a single courageous
step would carry us clear through them.   BRENDAN FRANCIS

Panic at the thought of doing a thing is a challenge to do it.
                                               HENRY S. HASKINS

Where man can find no answer, he will find fear. NORMAN COUSINS

FIRE

You may poke a man's fire after you've known him for seven years.
                                               ENGLISH PROVERB

One can enjoy a wood fire worthily only when he warms his
thoughts by it as well as his hands and his feet. ODELL SHEPHERD

What a friendly and companionable thing is a campfire! How
generous and outright it is! It plays for you when you wish to be
lively, and it glows for you when you wish to be reflective.
                                               DAVID GRAYSON

To poke a wood fire is more solid enjoyment than almost anything
else in the world.   CHARLES DUDLEY WARNER

People who light fires on the slightest provocation are always the
nicest. There's something comforting about fires.   JANE ENGLAND

FIRST LADY

Mrs. Hayes may not have much influence on Congress, but she has
great influence with me.   RUTHERFORD B. HAYES

The First Lady has no rules; rather, each new woman must make
her own.   SHANA ALEXANDER

Any First Lady will do all right if she is herself.   JOHN F. KENNEDY

Well, Warren Harding, I have got you the presidency; what are you
going to do with it?   FLORENCE HARDING,
                           to her husband on the day of his election

Oh, we talk about politics all the time. . . . Sometimes I really get

mean. . . . But I can be more helpful if I encourage him and don't
criticize.   ROSALYNN CARTER

When it was discovered that Mrs. [Dolley] Madison's ladylike
white fingers were tobacco-stained from habitually taking snuff, it
became chic for Washington ladies to take snuff also.

MARIANNE MEANS

Harry and I have been sweethearts and married more than forty
years—and no matter where I was, when I put out my hand,
Harry's was there to grasp it.   BESS TRUMAN

I had thought I would hate being First Lady. . . . I loved it.

BETTY FORD

Both the president and his wife can never give way to apprehen-
sion even though they are probably more aware than most citizens
of the dangers which may surround us. If the country is to be
confident, they must be confident.   ELEANOR ROOSEVELT

FISHING

There is no use in your walking five miles to fish when you can
depend on being just as unsuccessful near home.   MARK TWAIN

An angler is a man who spends rainy days sitting around on the
muddy banks of rivers doing nothing because his wife won't let
him do it at home.   IRISH NEWS

Fishermen don't lie. They just tell beautiful stories. SYNGMAN RHEE

The charm of fishing is that it is the pursuit of what is elusive but
attainable, a perpetual series of occasions for hope.   JOHN BUCHAN

There is peculiar pleasure in catching a trout in a place where
nobody thinks of looking for them, and at an hour when everybody
believes they cannot be caught.   HENRY VAN DYKE

The curious thing about fishing is you never want to go home. If
you catch something, you can't stop. If you don't catch anything,
you hate to leave in case something might bite.   GLADYS TABER

Fishing is a . . . discipline in the equality of men—for all men are
equal before fish.   HERBERT HOOVER

Bragging may not bring happiness, but no man having caught a large fish goes home through an alley.   ANONYMOUS

It has always been my private conviction that any man who pits his intelligence against a fish and loses has it coming.

JOHN STEINBECK

FLATTERY

Flattery rarely hurts a man unless he inhales.   ANONYMOUS

Flattery, if judiciously administered, is always acceptable, however much we may despise the flatterer. LADY MARGUERITE BLESSINGTON

I hate careless flattery, the kind that exhausts you in your effort to believe it.   WILSON MIZNER

Attention is a silent and perpetual flattery.   MADAME SWETCHINE

Words really flattering are not those which we prepare but those which escape us unthinkingly.   NINON DE LENCLOS

What really flatters a man is that you think him worth flattering.

GEORGE BERNARD SHAW

At the end of the day flattery and censure never know which has done the most harm.   HENRY S. HASKINS

What flatterers say try to make true.   GERMAN PROVERB

FOLLY

A good folly is worth whatever you pay for it.   GEORGE ADE

I believe more follies are committed out of complaisance to the world, than in following our own inclinations.

LADY MARY WORTLEY MONTAGU

He who hath not a dram of folly in his mixture hath pounds of much worse matter in his composition.   CHARLES LAMB

Meddling with another man's folly is always thankless work.

RUDYARD KIPLING

If folly were a pain, there would be groaning in every house.

BALTASAR GRACIAN

You will do foolish things, but do them with enthusiasm.

COLETTE

FOOD

Better to have bread and an onion with peace than stuffed fowl with strife.   ARAB PROVERB

In order to know whether a human being is young or old, offer it food of different kinds at short intervals. If young, it will eat anything at any hour of the day or night.   OLIVER WENDELL HOLMES

The longer I work in nutrition, the more convinced I become that for the healthy person all foods should be delicious.   ADELE DAVIS

The first of all considerations is that our meals shall be fun as well as fuel.   ANDRÉ SIMON

We connive to keep the calories down and feel triumphant when we get compliments on a low-calorie meal from the man we are trying to please.   LADY BIRD JOHNSON

My piece of bread only belongs to me when I know that everyone else has a share, and that no one starves while I eat.   LEO TOLSTOY

Never work before breakfast; if you have to work before breakfast, eat your breakfast first.   JOSH BILLINGS

Please, I wish you would have the cook give me only a six-ounce steak instead of the regular man-sized one. It's a terrible sentence the doctor has imposed on me.   WILLIAM HOWARD TAFT,
to the White House housekeeper

We are all dietetic sinners; only a small percent of what we eat nourishes us; the balance goes to waste and loss of energy.

SIR WILLIAM OSLER

At a dinner party one should eat wisely but not too well, and talk well but not too wisely.   W. SOMERSET MAUGHAM

FOOL

One is never so easily fooled as when one thinks one is fooling others.   LA ROCHEFOUCAULD

It is as idle to rage against man's fatuity as to hope that he will ever be less a fool.   GEORGE GISSING

Of the whole rabble of thieves, the fools are the worst; for they rob you of both time and peace of mind.   GOETHE

April 1. This is the day upon which we are reminded of what we are on the other three hundred and sixty-four.   MARK TWAIN

Most everyone seems willing to be a fool himself, but he can't bear to have anyone else one.   JOSH BILLINGS

A woman never forgives anybody who tries to keep her from making a fool of herself over a man.   JOHN W. RAPER

Luck sometimes visits a fool, but never sits down with him.

GERMAN PROVERB

FOOTBALL

You don't need a great offense to win a championship, but a great defense is a must.   FRAN TARKENTON

The NFL will have to adopt a hands-off policy on cheerleaders.

PETE ROZELLE

Never tell 'em how many letter men you've got coming back. Tell 'em how many you lost.   KNUTE ROCKNE

Speed is not your fastest, but your slowest man. No back can run faster than his interference.   JOCK SUTHERLAND

You're a hero when you win and a bum when you lose. That's the game.   JOHNNY UNITAS

There is no system of play that substitutes for knocking an opponent down. When you hit, hit hard.   POP WARNER

An atheist is a guy who watches a Notre Dame–SMU football game and doesn't care who wins.   DWIGHT D. EISENHOWER

I don't care anything about formations or new offenses or tricks on defense. You block and tackle better than the team you're playing, you win.   VINCE LOMBARDI

He was the only man I ever saw who ran his own interference.

STEVE OWEN,
on Bronko Nagurski

FORTUNE

Henceforth I ask not good-fortune, I myself am good-fortune.

WALT WHITMAN

If fortune smiles, who doesn't? If fortune doesn't, who does?

CHINESE PROVERB

He who finds Fortune on his side should go briskly ahead, for she is wont to favor the bold.   BALTASAR GRACIAN

Fortune is like the market, where many times, if you can stay a little, the price will fall.   FRANCIS BACON

I have always believed that all things depended upon Fortune and nothing upon ourselves.   LORD BYRON

A day of fortune is like a harvest day; we must be busy when the corn is ripe.   GOETHE

FRANCE AND THE FRENCH

The French are difficult people. You have to speak the language terribly well, otherwise they can take advantage of you. JANE FONDA

What is not clear is not French.   COMTE DE RIVAROL

It may be the only country in the world where the rich are sometimes brilliant.   LILLIAN HELLMAN

How can you be expected to govern a country that has 246 kinds of cheese?   CHARLES DE GAULLE

Like all self-controlled people, the French talk to themselves.

F. SCOTT FITZGERALD

FREEDOM

It requires greater courage to preserve inner freedom, to move on in one's inward journey into new realms, than to stand defiantly for outer freedom.   ROLLO MAY

Those who expect to reap the blessings of freedom must, like men, undergo the fatigues of supporting it.   THOMAS JEFFERSON

There is no surer way to give men the courage to be free than to insure them a competence upon which they can rely.

WALTER LIPPMANN

Freedom is nothing else but a chance to be better, whereas enslavement is a certainty of the worst.   ALBERT CAMUS

Freedom lies in being bold.   ROBERT FROST

We feel free when we escape—even if it be but from the frying pan into the fire.   ERIC HOFFER

Freedom, especially a woman's freedom, is a conquest to be made, not a gift to be received. It isn't granted. It must be taken.

FEDERICO FELLINI

FRIEND AND FRIENDSHIP

Probably no man ever had a friend that he did not dislike a little.

E. W. HOWE

There are deep sorrows and killing cares in life, but the encouragement and love of friends were given us to make all difficulties bearable.   JOHN OLIVER HOBBES

Here's a dime. Call all your friends.   TOM MEANY,
to an unpopular sportswriter

You can hardly make a friend in a year, but you can lose one in an hour.   CHINESE PROVERB

One doesn't know, till one is a bit at odds with the world, how much one's friends who believe in one rather generously, mean to one.   D. H. LAWRENCE

Many a one cannot loosen his own fetters, but is nevertheless his friend's emancipator.   FRIEDRICH NIETZSCHE

Keep your friendships in repair.   RALPH WALDO EMERSON

The paths of social advancement are strewn with shattered friendships.   H. G. WELLS

The friend who understands you, creates you.   ROMAIN ROLLAND

FUTURE

I never think of the future. It comes soon enough. ALBERT EINSTEIN

It is the business of the future to be dangerous.
ALFRED NORTH WHITEHEAD

We should all be concerned about the future because we will have to spend the rest of our lives there.   CHARLES F. KETTERING

Perhaps the best thing about the future is that it only comes one day at a time.   DEAN ACHESON

The most effective way to ensure the value of the future is to confront the present courageously and constructively.   ROLLO MAY

History is apt to judge harshly those who sacrifice tomorrow for today.   HAROLD MACMILLAN

No one knows the story of tomorrow's dawn.   AFRICAN PROVERB

We grow in time to trust the future for our answers. RUTH BENEDICT

GAMBLING

The urge to gamble is so universal and its practice so pleasurable that I assume it must be evil.   HEYWOOD HALE BROUN

Gambling: The sure way of getting nothing for something.
WILSON MIZNER

Nine gamblers could not feed a single rooster.   YUGOSLAV PROVERB

If you won't gamble enough to hurt you, it won't do you any good to win.   BILL LEAR

Remember this: The house doesn't beat a player. It merely gives him the opportunity to beat himself.
NICHOLAS ("NICK THE GREEK") DANDALOS

Gaming is the son of avarice, and the father of despair.
FRENCH PROVERB

Why they call a fellow that keeps losing all the time a good sport gets me.   KIN HUBBARD

GARDENS AND GARDENING

One of the most delightful things about a garden is the anticipation it provides.   W. E. JOHNS

Our vegetable garden is coming along well, with radishes and beans up, and we are less worried about revolution than we used to be.   E. B. WHITE

When you have done your best for a flower, and it fails, you have some reason to be aggrieved.   FRANK SWINNERTON

I have never had so many good ideas day after day as when I worked in the garden.   JOHN ERSKINE

Men can't be trusted with pruning shears any more than they can be trusted with the grocery money in a delicatessen. . . . They are like boys with new pocket knives who will not stop whittling.

PHYLLIS MC GINLEY

Let no one think that real gardening is a bucolic and meditative occupation. It is an insatiable passion, like everything else to which a man gives his heart.   KAREL ČAPEK

It is a consoling thought that gardens and their laws of birth and death endure, while political crises and panaceas appear only to vanish.   VIDA D. SCUDDER

GENIUS

It is the essence of genius to make use of the simplest ideas.

CHARLES PÉGUY

When James McNeill Whistler, the painter, was asked if he thought genius hereditary, he replied, "I can't tell you; heaven has granted me no offspring."   HESKETH PEARSON

The genius so-called is only that one who discerns the pattern of things within the confusion of details a little sooner than the average man.   BEN SHAHN

Genius is the capacity of evading hard work.   ELBERT HUBBARD

Genius, by its very intensity, decrees a special path of fire for its vivid power.   PHILLIPS BROOKS

It's quite impossible to believe that a man is a genius, if you've been to school with him, or even known his father.

ARNOLD BENNETT

With talent, you do what you like. With genius, you do what you can.

JEAN INGRES

The function of genius is not to give new answers, but pose new questions which time and mediocrity can resolve.

H. R. TREVOR-ROPER

Men give me credit for genius; but all the genius I have lies in this: When I have a subject on hand I study it profoundly.

ALEXANDER HAMILTON

The barriers are not yet erected which can say to aspiring genius: "Thus far and no further."

LUDWIG VON BEETHOVEN

GIFT

It's sweet to be remembered, but it's often cheaper to be forgotten.

KIN HUBBARD

What was least expected is the more highly esteemed.

BALTASAR GRACIAN

He is very fond of making things which he doesn't want, and then giving them to people who have no use for them.

ANTHONY HOPE

It helped her learn that something you create yourself is the best kind of present.

JACQUELINE KENNEDY,
*referring to a Christmas card that her daughter,
Caroline, had made for President Kennedy*

There is only one real deprivation, I decided this morning, and that is not to be able to give gifts to those one loves most.

MAY SARTON

What is bought is cheaper than a gift.   PORTUGUESE PROVERB

To receive a present handsomely and in a right spirit, even when you have none to give in return, is to give one in return.

LEIGH HUNT

What's your rule for choosing a present? Mine is, would I like it?

Who knows what anyone else likes, but if I like it, that at least is something.   RUTH GORDON

GIVING

Blessed are those who can give without remembering, and take without forgetting.   ELIZABETH BIBESCO

No person was ever honored for what he received; honor has been the reward for what he gave.   CALVIN COOLIDGE

People that pay for things never complain. It's the guy you give something to that you can't please.   WILL ROGERS

Things of the spirit differ from things material in that the more you give the more you have.   CHRISTOPHER MORLEY

Sometimes a man imagines that he will lose himself if he gives himself, and keep himself if he hides himself. But the contrary takes place with terrible exactitude.   ERNEST HELLO

Is devotion to others a cover for the hungers and the needs of the self, of which one is ashamed? I was always ashamed to take. So I gave. It was not a virtue. It was a disguise.   ANAÏS NIN

Giving is the highest expression of potency.   ERICH FROMM

GOD

The Great Spirit, in placing men on the earth, desired them to take good care of the ground and to do each other no harm.

YOUNG CHIEF,
of the Cayuses

I never really look for anything. What God throws my way comes. I wake up in the morning and whichever way God turns my feet, I go.   PEARL BAILEY

I have never understood why it should be considered derogatory to the Creator to suppose that he has a sense of humor.

WILLIAM R. INGE

God is for men and religion for women.   JOSEPH CONRAD

When you knock, ask to see God—none of the servants.

HENRY DAVID THOREAU

As to God, open your eyes—and your heart, which is also a perceptive organ—and you see him.   CHARLES SANDERS PEIRCE

God delays but doesn't forget.   SPANISH PROVERB

Apart from God every activity is merely a passing whiff of insignificance.   ALFRED NORTH WHITEHEAD

The true God, the strong God, is the God of ideas. ALFRED DE VIGNY

God gave burdens, also shoulders.   YIDDISH PROVERB

An atheist may be simply one whose faith and love are concentrated on the impersonal aspects of God.   SIMONE WEIL

It does me no injury for my neighbor to say there are twenty gods or no God. It neither picks my pocket nor breaks my leg.
THOMAS JEFFERSON

GOLF

Golf is a wonderful exercise. You can stand on your feet for hours, watching somebody else putt.   WILL ROGERS

When you're too old to chase other things, you can always chase golf balls.   ANONYMOUS

Serenity is knowing that your worst shot is still going to be pretty good.   JOHNNY MILLER

Golf is essentially an exercise in masochism conducted out-of-doors.   PAUL O'NEIL

When I hit a ball, I want someone else to go chase it.
ROGER HORNSBY

Old golfers never die; they just lose their balls.   ANONYMOUS

The average golfer doesn't play golf. He attacks it.   JACK BURKE

I'm playing like Tarzan—and scoring like Jane. CHI CHI RODRIGUEZ

GOOD

No people do more harm than those who go about doing good.
BISHOP CREIGHTON

He who waits to do a great deal of good at once, will never do anything.   SAMUEL JOHNSON

There are bad people who would be less dangerous if they were quite devoid of goodness.   LA ROCHEFOUCAULD

It we shall take the good we find, asking no questions, we shall have heaping measures.   RALPH WALDO EMERSON

Nothing can be more readily disproved than the old saw, "You can't keep a good man down." Most human societies have been beautifully organized to keep good men down.   JOHN W. GARDNER

If you love the good that you see in another, you make it your own.   SAINT GREGORY THE GREAT

I know what things are good: friendship and work and conversation. These I shall have.   RUPERT BROOKE

Modern spiritual exercises ought to include a ten-minute meditation on the goodness of man.   ROBERT C. POLLOCK

On the whole, human beings want to be good, but not too good, and not quite all the time.   GEORGE ORWELL

GOSSIP

Gossip is the opiate of the oppressed.   ERICA JONG

Men have always detested women's gossip because they suspect the truth: Their measurements are being taken and compared.   ERICA JONG

If you want to get the most out of life why the thing to do is to be a gossiper by day and a gossipee by night.   OGDEN NASH

Who brings a tale takes two away.   IRISH PROVERB

Gossip is the art of saying nothing in a way that leaves practically nothing unsaid.   ANONYMOUS

There is only one thing worse than being talked about, and that is not being talked about.   OSCAR WILDE

GOVERNMENT

Government is not a substitute for people, but simply the instrument through which they act. And if the individual fails to do his duty as a citizen, government becomes a very deadly instrument indeed.   BERNARD M. BARUCH

Better the occasional faults of a government that lives in a spirit of charity than the consistent omissions of a government frozen in the ice of its own indifference.   FRANKLIN D. ROOSEVELT

The best minds are not in government. If any were, business would hire them away.   RONALD REAGAN

Even a fool can govern if nothing happens.   GERMAN PROVERB

When one is in office one has no idea how damnable things can feel to the ordinary rank and file of the public.

SIR WINSTON CHURCHILL

My experience in government is that when things are non-controversial, beautifully coordinated, and all the rest, it must be that there is not much going on.   JOHN F. KENNEDY

The art of government cannot be gotten out of books. Try, make mistakes, learn how to govern.   NIKOLAI LENIN

GRANDPARENTS

The closest friends I have made all through life have been people who also grew up close to a loved and loving grandmother or grandfather.   MARGARET MEAD

If you would civilize a man, begin with his grandmother.

VICTOR HUGO

Grandparents are frequently more congenial with their grand-children than with their children.   ANDRÉ MAUROIS

Once your children are grown up and have children of their own, the problems are theirs and the less the older generation interferes the better.   ELEANOR ROOSEVELT

Was there ever a grandparent, bushed after a day of minding noisy youngsters, who hasn't felt the Lord knew what He was doing when He gave little children to young people?   JOE E. WELLS

GRATITUDE

Ingratitude is always a form of weakness. I have never known a man of real ability to be ungrateful.   GOETHE

Who does not thank for little will not thank for much.

ESTONIAN PROVERB

We have all known ingratitude, ungrateful we have never been.

DIANE DE POITIERS

One finds little ingratitude so long as one is in a position to grant favors.   FRENCH PROVERB

Never thank anybody for anything, except a drink of water in the desert—and then make it brief.   GENE FOWLER

There is no gratitude for things past. Gratitude is always for what you're going to do for people in the future.   HARRY S. TRUMAN

GREATNESS

The greatest men are always linked to their age by some weakness or other.   GOETHE

Few great men could pass personnel.   PAUL GOODMAN

Great men taken in any way are profitable company.

THOMAS CARLYLE

Really great men have a curious feeling that the greatness is not in them but through them.   JOHN RUSKIN

To feel themselves in the presence of true greatness many men find it necessary only to be alone.   TOM MASSON

I have learned the truth of the observation that the more one approaches great men the more one finds that they are men.

BERNARD M. BARUCH

Altogether it will be found that a quiet life is characteristic of great men, and that their pleasures have not been of the sort that would look exciting to the outward eye.   BERTRAND RUSSELL

The greatest man who ever came out of Plymouth Corner, Vermont.   CLARENCE DARROW,
on Calvin Coolidge

We are always glad when a great man reassures us of his humanity by possessing a few peculiarities.   ANDRÉ MAUROIS

To achieve great things, we must live as though we were never going to die.   VAUVENARGUES

The greater a man is, the more distasteful is praise and flattery to him.   JOHN BURROUGHS

GROWTH

To teach a man how he may learn to grow independently, and for himself, is perhaps the greatest service that one man can do to another.   BENJAMIN JOWETT

Growth is demanding and may seem dangerous, for there is loss as well as gain in growth. But why go on living if one has ceased to grow?   MAY SARTON

No man fears what he has seen grow.   AFRICAN PROVERB

You must grow like a tree, not like a mushroom.
                                        JANET ERSKINE STUART

What grows makes no noise.   GERMAN PROVERB

Growth, in some curious way, I suspect, depends on being always in motion just a little bit, one way or another.   NORMAN MAILER

You've got to do your own growing, no matter how tall your grandfather was.   IRISH PROVERB

Each forward step we take we leave some phantom of ourselves behind.   JOHN LANCASTER SPALDING

GUEST

People are either born hosts or born guests.   SIR MAX BEERBOHM

I always feel that I have two duties to perform with a parting guest: one, to see that he doesn't forget anything that is his; the other, to see that he doesn't take anything that is mine.
                                        ALFRED NORTH WHITEHEAD

I've had a wonderful evening—but this wasn't it.   GROUCHO MARX,
                                        to a Hollywood hostess

Nobody can be as agreeable as an uninvited guest.   KIN HUBBARD

Some people can stay longer in an hour than others can in a week.
                                        WILLIAM DEAN HOWELLS

It's what the guests say as they swing out of the driveway that counts.   ANONYMOUS

He who is loathe to leave shakes hands often.   FRENCH PROVERB

Staying with people consists in your not having your own way, and their not having theirs.   MAARTEN MAARTENS

If it were not for guests all houses would be graves. KAHLIL GIBRAN

HABIT

A man will pursue his habit to his death rather than change it.
RICHARD JEFFERIES

A man may have no bad habits and have worse.   MARK TWAIN

A very slight change in our habits is sufficient to destroy our sense of our daily reality, and the reality of the world about us.
GEORGE MOORE

Bad habits are easier to abandon today than tomorrow.
YIDDISH PROVERB

Habit is a man's sole comfort. We dislike doing without even unpleasant things to which we have become accustomed.   GOETHE

Habit and routine have an unbelievable power to waste and destroy.   HENRI DE LUBAC

Every grown-up man consists wholly of habits, although he is often unaware of it and even denies having any habits at all.
GEORGES GURDJIEFF

You see what will happen if you keep biting your nails.
NOEL COWARD,
*on a postcard which had a statue
of the Venus de Milo*

HAPPINESS

Most folks are about as happy as they make up their minds to be.
ABRAHAM LINCOLN

Happiness is a form of courage.   HOLBROOK JACKSON

It's pretty hard to tell what does bring happiness. Poverty and wealth have both failed.   KIN HUBBARD

When one door of happiness closes another opens; but often we look so long at the closed door that we do not see the one which has been opened for us.   HELEN KELLER

The first thing to learn in intercourse with others is noninterference with their own peculiar ways of being happy, provided those ways do not assume to interfere by violence with ours.

WILLIAM JAMES

The purpose of life is not to be happy—but to *matter,* to be productive, to be useful, to have it make some difference that you have lived at all.   LEO ROSTEN

In every part and corner of our life, to lose oneself is to be the gainer; to forget oneself is to be happy.   ROBERT LOUIS STEVENSON

It is one of my sources of happiness never to desire a knowledge of other people's business.   DOLLEY MADISON

Happiness is the interval between periods of unhappiness.

DON MARQUIS

On the whole, the happiest people seem to be those who have no particular cause for being happy except that they are so.

WILLIAM R. INGE

Happiness is not a goal, it is a by-product.   ELEANOR ROOSEVELT

Happiness springs from intense activity in congenial surroundings.

HAROLD NICHOLSON

If ignorance is bliss, why aren't there more happy people?

ANONYMOUS

One of the oldest and quietest roads to contentment lies through the conventional trinity of wine, woman, and song.

REXFORD GUY TUGWELL

The greatest happiness is to be that which one is. THEODORE HERZL

HATE

Everybody ought to do at least two things each day that he hates to do, just for practice.   WILLIAM JAMES

There is no medicine to cure hatred.   AFRICAN PROVERB

It is because people do not know each other that they hate each other so little.   REMY DE GOURMONT

Next to genius, nothing is more clear-sighted than hatred.
CLAUDE BERNARD

We hate what we fear and so where hate is, fear is lurking.
CYRIL CONNOLLY

Hate must make a man productive. Otherwise one might as well love.   KARL KRAUS

Man is a hating rather than a loving animal.   REBECCA WEST

HEALTH

See the pale color of my face and do not ask after my health.
PERSIAN PROVERB

I won't say I'm out of condition now—but I even puff going downstairs.   DICK GREGORY

A man needs a purpose for real health.   SHERWOOD ANDERSON

All sorts of bodily diseases are produced by half-used minds.
GEORGE BERNARD SHAW

Those obsessed with health are not healthy; the first requisite of good health is a certain calculated carelessness about oneself.
SYDNEY J. HARRIS

Health without wealth is half a sickness.   THOMAS FULLER

Health is the thing that makes you feel that now is the best time of the year.   FRANKLIN P. ADAMS

Health of body and mind is a great blessing, if we can bear it.
JOHN HENRY CARDINAL NEWMAN

There's lots of people in this world who spend so much time watching their health that they haven't the time to enjoy it.
JOSH BILLINGS

HEART

Hardness of heart is a dreadful quality, but it is doubtful whether in the long run it works more damage than softness of head.

THEODORE ROOSEVELT

Faces we see, hearts we know not.   SPANISH PROVERB

Every time a man unburdens his heart to a stranger he reaffirms the love that unites humanity.   GERMAINE GREER

There's only one way of being happy by the heart: namely, to have none.   PAUL BOURGET

It is not by the gray of the hair that one knows the age of the heart.

EDWARD BULWER-LYTTON

It is only with the heart that one can see rightly; what is essential is invisible to the eye.   ANTOINE DE SAINT-EXUPÉRY

HELP

There are people in life, and there are many of them, whom you will have to help as long as they live. They will never be able to stand alone.   SIR WILLIAM OSLER

To help all created things, that is the measure of our responsibility; to be helped by all, that is the measure of our hope.   GERALD VANN

Mistrust your zeal for doing good to others.   ABBÉ HUVELIN

When one is helping another, both are strong.   GERMAN PROVERB

It is hideous and coarse to assume that we can do something for others—and it is vile not to endeavor to do it.   EDWARD DAHLBERG

The *healthy* and *strong* individual is the one who asks for help when he needs it. Whether he's got an abscess on his knee or in his soul.

RONA BARRETT

HERO

It is the next century that, looking over its own, will see the heroes of our own time clearly.   RUDYARD KIPLING

People are hungry for a hero, one who fits the new age. . . . A good deal is riding on the question whether they will find a demagogue or a democrat as they search out a way to link their passions to their government.   JAMES DAVID BARBER

A hero is one who does what he can. ROMAIN ROLLAND

Being a hero is about the shortest-lived profession on earth.
WILL ROGERS

Heroism consists in hanging on one minute longer.
NORWEGIAN PROVERB

As you get older, it is harder to have heroes, but it is sort of necessary. ERNEST HEMINGWAY

HISTORY

The only thing we learn from history is that we do not learn.
EARL WARREN

No one makes history: One doesn't see it happen, any more than we see the grass grow. BORIS PASTERNAK

History never looks like history when you are living through it. It always looks confusing and messy, and it always feels uncomfortable. JOHN W. GARDNER

It is not the neutrals or the lukewarms who make history.
ADOLF HITLER

The best that history has to give us is the enthusiasm which it arouses. GOETHE

The great tragedies of history occur not when right confronts wrong, but when two rights confront each other.
HENRY A. KISSINGER

Historians may lie but history cannot. GEORGE SAINTSBURY

HOME

One's own surroundings mean so much to one, when one is feeling miserable. EDITH SITWELL

The first thing in one's home is comfort; let beauty of detail be added if one has the means, the patience, the eye. GEORGE GISSING

A man's home may be his castle on the outside; inside, it is more often his nursery. CLARE BOOTH LUCE

No matter how much a man likes his own home, a week or so by himself in a hotel room can be pretty nice, every year or so.

JOHN MC NULTY

Better to be kind at home than burn incense in a far place.

CHINESE PROVERB

The fellow that owns his own home is always just coming out of a hardware store.   KIN HUBBARD

HOPE

Hope is the only universal liar who never loses his reputation for veracity.   ROBERT G. INGERSOLL

The mind which renounces, once and forever, a futile hope, has its compensation in ever-growing calm.   GEORGE GISSING

More are taken in by hope than by cunning.   VAUVENARGUES

I am a little deaf, a little blind, a little impotent, and on top of this are two or three abominable infirmities, but nothing destroys my hope.   VOLTAIRE

Hope is bad for the happy man, and good for the unhappy.

LEO TOLSTOY

HORSE RACING

The more horse sense a fellow has the less he bets on 'em.

KIN HUBBARD

A race track is a place where windows clean people. DANNY THOMAS

The people who think they can wind up ahead of the races are everybody who has ever won a bet.   OGDEN NASH

Never back the horses you admire most, for the horses you admire never win races.   J. A. SPENDER

Horse racing is animated roulette.   ROGER KAHN

HOUSE

Early relative—things my relatives gave me.   SHELLEY WINTERS,
when asked how her house was furnished

Every woman knows that it isn't what you do in a house that shows, but what you don't do.   MARCELENE COX

Unless one decorates one's house for oneself alone, best leave it bare, for other people are walleyed.   D. H. LAWRENCE

A house that does not have one worn, comfy chair in it is soulless.
MAY SARTON

Houses reveal character.   GILBERT HIGHET

Anybody who has any doubt about the ingenuity or the resourcefulness of a plumber never got any bill from one.   GEORGE MEANY

You sometimes see a woman who would have made a Joan of Arc in another century and climate, threshing herself to pieces over all the mean worry of housekeeping.   RUDYARD KIPLING

HUMOR

All humor, basically, is based on conflict.   NORMAN LEAR

Generally speaking, I don't believe in kindly humor. I don't think it exists.   S. J. PERELMAN

Men will take almost any kind of criticism except the observation that they have no sense of humor.   STEVE ALLEN

Someone once defined humor as a way to keep from killing yourself. I keep my sense of humor and I stay alive.   ABE BURROWS

Humor is as personal as sex.   JEAN SHEPHERD

A dirty joke is not, of course, a serious attack upon morality, but it is a sort of mental rebellion, a momentary wish that things were otherwise.   GEORGE ORWELL

Nothing is more curious than the almost savage hostility that humor excites in those who lack it.   GEORGE SAINTSBURY

HUNTING

When a man wants to murder a tiger he calls it sport: when the tiger wants to murder him he calls it ferocity.

GEORGE BERNARD SHAW

The deer season just opened. A deer hunter in Ventura County brought in his first man yesterday.   WILL ROGERS

One can foresee the consequences of a revolution or a war, but it is impossible to foresee the consequences of an autumn shooting-trip for wild ducks.   LEON TROTSKY

It is not every day that daddy kills a deer.   IRISH PROVERB

To the hunter a gun is what a pen is to a writer. One must have one's own pen for writing—and one's own gun for shooting.

LAURENS VAN DER POST

HURRY

God made time, but man made haste.   IRISH PROVERB

If you must be in a hurry, then let it be according to the old adage, and hasten slowly.   SAINT VINCENT DE PAUL

He is invariably in a hurry. Being in a hurry is one of the tributes he pays to life.   ELIZABETH BIBESCO

He who is in a hurry rides on a donkey.   GERMAN PROVERB

Whoever is in a hurry shows that the thing he is about is too big for him.   LORD CHESTERFIELD

HUSBAND

A husband is what is left of the lover after the nerve has been extracted.   HELEN ROWLAND

An ideal husband is one who treats his wife like a new car.

DAN BENNET

It makes a wife shudder to think what bad habits her husband might acquire if he did not smoke, drink, and swear.   ANONYMOUS

My husband will never chase another woman. He's too fine, too decent, too old.   GRACIE ALLEN

I won't say that a woman cannot have a fancy for her husband— after all, he is a man.   GERARD DE NERVAL

In Madagascar, women pay homage to their husbands by licking their feet.   HENRY THOMAS BUCKLE

Do not put such unlimited power in the hands of husbands. . . . Remember all men would be tyrants if they could. ABIGAIL ADAMS,
advice to her husband, who was
helping to draw up the first code
of laws at the Continental Congress

Husbands are like fires. They go out when unattended.
                                              ZSA ZSA GABOR

Women seem to be all right on bargains till it comes to picking out a husband.   KIN HUBBARD

The majority of husbands remind me of an orangutan trying to play the violin.   HONORÉ DE BALZAC

You know, women always could endure more than men. Not only physically, but mentally—did you ever get a peek at some of the husbands?   WILL ROGERS

Most wives think of their husbands as bumbling braggarts with whom they happen to be in love.   JACKIE GLEASON

A woman must always know more about her husband than he thinks she knows, and more than he knows about himself.
                                        MRS. ALBERT EINSTEIN

A husband is one who stands by you in troubles you wouldn't have had if you hadn't married him.   ANONYMOUS

Any husband who really cares for his wife will naturally help her in any way he can.   ELEANOR ROOSEVELT

American women expect to find in their husbands a perfection that English women only hope to find in their butlers.
                                      W. SOMERSET MAUGHAM

I can't think of anything more boring than to be married to a nice complacent husband.   DAME SYBIL THORNDIKE

IDEA

What matters is not the idea a man holds, but the depth at which he holds it.   EZRA POUND

An idea isn't responsible for the people who believe it.
                                    DON MARQUIS

With all the mass media concentrated in a few hands, the ancient faith in the competition of ideas in the free market seems like a hollow echo of a much simpler day.   KINGMAN BREWSTER, JR.

The only valid censorship of ideas is the right of people not to listen.   TOMMY SMOTHERS

One of the greatest pains to human nature is the pain of a new idea.   WALTER BAGEHOT

Very simple ideas are within the reach of only very complicated minds.   REMY DE GOURMONT

There is no defense, except stupidity, against the impact of a new idea.   PERCY W. BRIDGMAN

IDEAL

When a man forgets his ideals he may hope for happiness, but not till then.   JOHN OLIVER HOBBES

Every moral or social ideal indicates the presence of better conditions which are trying to break through and become the rule of life.
                                    HENRY FORD

Some people never have anything except ideals.   E. W. HOWE

If an ideal is possible it must already be in the thoughts of the people.   ROBERT LOUIS STEVENSON

Our ideals, like the gods of old, are constantly demanding human sacrifices.   GEORGE BERNARD SHAW

IDLENESS

To do great work a man must be very idle as well as very industrious.   SAMUEL BUTLER

To be idle requires a strong sense of personal identity.

ROBERT LOUIS STEVENSON

How beautiful it is to do nothing, and then to rest afterward.

SPANISH PROVERB

Idleness is not doing nothing; idleness is *being free to do anything*.

FLOYD DELL

Loafing needs no explanation and is its own excuse.

CHRISTOPHER MORLEY

IGNORANCE

To be ignorant of one's ignorance is the malady of ignorance.

A. BRONSON ALCOTT

The pleasures of ignorance are as great, in their way, as the pleasures of knowledge.   ALDOUS HUXLEY

Your ignorance cramps my conversation.   ANTHONY HOPE

A man's ignorance is as much a part of the instinctive art of his life as any learning he may acquire.   JOHN COWPER POWYS

It takes a lot of things to prove you are smart, but only one thing to prove you are ignorant.   DON HEROLD

ILLNESS

The worst thing about medicine is that one kind makes another necessary.   ELBERT HUBBARD

If you're a hypochondriac, first class, you awaken each morning with the firm resolve not to worry; everything is going to turn out all wrong.   GOODMAN ACE

If the patient dies, the doctor killed him; if he gets well, the saints cured him.   GERMAN PROVERB

The modern sympathy with invalids is morbid. Illness of any kind is hardly a thing to encourage in others.   OSCAR WILDE

The desire to take medicine is perhaps the greatest feature which distinguishes man from animals.   SIR WILLIAM OSLER

Men make use of their illnesses at least as much as they are made use of by them.   ALDOUS HUXLEY

What poor things does a fever-fit or an overflowing of the bile make of the masters of creation!   SIR WALTER SCOTT

Every disease is a physician.   IRISH PROVERB

To feel keenly the poetry of a morning's roses, one has to have just escaped from the claws of this vulture which we call sickness.
HENRI FREDERIC AMIEL

IMITATION

Almost all absurdity of conduct arises from the imitation of those whom we cannot resemble.   SAMUEL JOHNSON

The ass went seeking for horns and lost his ears.   ARAB PROVERB

Most of the things we do, we do for no better reason than that our fathers have done them or that our neighbors do them, and the same is true of a larger part than we suspect of what we think.
OLIVER WENDELL HOLMES, JR.

One dog barks at something, and a hundred bark at the sound.
CHINESE PROVERB

When people are free to do as they please, they usually imitate each other.   ERIC HOFFER

IMMORTALITY

I suppose that everyone of us hopes secretly for immortality; to leave, I mean, a name behind him which will live forever in this world, whatever he may be doing, himself, in the next. A. A. MILNE

Without love, immortality would be frightful and horrible.
THEODOR HAECKER

Let him who believes in immortality enjoy his happiness in silence, without giving himself airs about it.   GOETHE

I [have] often said that the best argument I knew for an immortal life was the existence of a man who deserved one.   WILLIAM JAMES

IMPOSSIBLE

An impossibility does not disturb us until its accomplishment shows what fools we were.   HENRY S. HASKINS

You write, "It is impossible": That is not French.

NAPOLEON BONAPARTE

By asking for the impossible we obtain the best possible.

ITALIAN PROVERB

Men will never cease to attempt the impossible and to assault the impregnable.   W. MACNEILE DIXON

Few things are impossible in themselves; application to make them succeed fails us more often than the means.   LA ROCHEFOUCAULD

INDEPENDENCE

Woman will be the last one on earth to learn independence, to find strength in herself.   ANAÏS NIN

It's the man who dares to take who is independent, not he who gives.   D. H. LAWRENCE

Men are made stronger on realization that the helping hand they need is at the end of their own right arm.   SIDNEY J. PHILLIPS

You can listen to what everybody says, but the fact remains that you've got to get out there and do the thing yourself.

JOAN SUTHERLAND

There is a great deal of self-will in the world, but very little genuine independence of character.   FREDERICK W. FABER

Independence is for the very few; it is a privilege of the strong.

FRIEDRICH NIETZSCHE

INDIANS

I don't blame our Indians for being discouraged. They are the only ones to be conquered by the United States and not come out ahead.   HARRY OLIVER

[The Indian] sees no need for setting apart one day in seven as a holy day, since to him all days are God's.   OHIYESA,
of the Santee Dakotas

I can still see the butchered women and children lying heaped and scattered. . . . And I can see that something else died there in the bloody mud. . . . A people's dream died there.   BLACK ELK

My ancestors didn't come over on the *Mayflower*—they met the boat.   WILL ROGERS

What is necessary is that whoever wishes to know the Indian must go to the Indian. Not to visit, but to live. Not to judge, but to learn.   STAN STEINER

So the Indian record is the bearer of one great message to the world. Through his society, and only through his society, man experiences greatness; through it he unites with the universe and God, and through it, he is freed from all fear.   JOHN COLLIER

INDIVIDUALISM

If you wish to understand others you must intensify your own individualism.   OSCAR WILDE

I've always thought that the power of any country is the sum of the total of its individuals. Each individual rich with ideas, with concepts, rich with his own revolution.   RAY BRADBURY

"Do you know what individuality is?"
"No."
"Consciousness of will. To be conscious that you have a will and can act."
Yes, it is. It's a glorious saying.   KATHERINE MANSFIELD

Nonconformism is the major, perhaps the only, sin of our time.   ROBERT LINDER

Whatever crushes individuality is despotism, by whatever name it may be called.   JOHN STUART MILL

Individualism is rather like innocence; there must be something unconscious about it.   LOUIS KRONENBERGER

We talk much more about individualism and liberty than our ancestors. But as so often happens, when anything becomes conscious, the consciousness is compensatory for absence in practice.

JOHN DEWEY

Each individual thinks himself the center of the world. Nothing seems more important to us than our own existence. ALEXIS CARREL

INFLATION

If inflation continues to soar, you're going to have to work like a dog just to live like one.   GEORGE GOBEL

A nickel ain't worth a dime anymore.   YOGI BERRA

Inflation cannot be vanquished without effort and sacrifice. . . . There are no simple solutions, no magic wands to wave inflation away.   JIMMY CARTER

In the old days a man who saved money was a miser; nowadays he's a wonder.   ANONYMOUS

Inflation? I don't know what it's all about. I don't know any more about this than an economist does, and God knows, he don't know anything!   WILL ROGERS

It is all very well to blame inflation on the government, but isn't it caused fundamentally by our selfishness and self-indulgence?

BERNARD M. BARUCH

INFLUENCE

Human beings are not influenced by anything to which they are not naturally disposed.   HESKETH PEARSON

You can exert no influence if you are not susceptible to influence.

CARL G. JUNG

If I am not pleased with myself, but should wish to be other than I am, why should I think highly of the influences which have made me what I am?   JOHN LANCASTER SPALDING

He who goes with wolves learns to howl.   SPANISH PROVERB

Why are there men and women that while they are nigh me the sunlight expands my blood? Why when they leave me do my pennants of joy sink flat and lank?   WALT WHITMAN

One of the things a man has to learn to fight most bitterly is the influence of those who love him.   SHERWOOD ANDERSON

INFORMATION

Reports in matters of this world are many, and our resources of mind for the discrimination of them very insufficient.

JOHN HENRY CARDINAL NEWMAN

Often, the surest way to convey misinformation is to tell the strict truth.   MARK TWAIN

A merely well-informed man is the most useless bore on God's earth.   ALFRED NORTH WHITEHEAD

We have smothered ourselves, buried ourselves, in the vast heap of information which all of us have and none of us has.

GAMALIEL BRADFORD

Some men will never ask for information, because it implies that they do not know.   HENRY CARDINAL MANNING

O, what a brave thing it is, in every case and circumstance of a matter, to be thoroughly well-informed!   RABELAIS

INSPIRATION

Inspiration always comes when a man wills it, but it does not always depart when he wishes.   CHARLES BAUDELAIRE

Just as appetite comes by eating, so work brings inspiration, if inspiration is not discernible at the beginning.   IGOR STRAVINSKY

Inspirations never go in for long engagements; they demand immediate marriage to action.   BRENDAN FRANCIS

The most beautiful thing in the world is, precisely, the conjunction of learning and inspiration.   WANDA LANDOWSKA

There is no inspiration in the ideals of plenty and stability.

JOHN LANCASTER SPALDING

Something tells me needs only decent attention and confidence to tell much more.   HENRY S. HASKINS

INTELLIGENCE

Intelligence is characterized by a natural inability to understand life.   HENRI BERGSON

Everyone speaks well of his heart, but no one dares to say it of his head.   LA ROCHEFOUCAULD

True intelligence very readily conceives of an intelligence superior to its own; and this is why truly intelligent men are modest.
ANDRÉ GIDE

The amount of intelligence necessary to please us is a most accurate measure of the amount of intelligence we have ourselves.
HELVÉTIUS

Intelligence is quickness in seeing things as they are.
GEORGE SANTAYANA

A great many people think that polysyllables are a sign of intelligence.   BARBARA WALTERS

INTEREST

The minute a man is convinced that he's interesting, he isn't.
STEPHEN LEACOCK

Interests are anchors, and I believe they will bring peace and even happiness in the end.   A. C. BENSON

When you are genuinely interested in one thing it will always lead to something else.   ELEANOR ROOSEVELT

I don't know if I should care for a man who made life easy; I should want someone who made it interesting.   EDITH WHARTON

In the ideal sense nothing is uninteresting; there are only uninterested people.   BROOKS ATKINSON

IRELAND AND THE IRISH

The quiet Irishman is about as harmless as a powder magazine built over a match factory.   JAMES DUNNE

The Irish do not want anyone to wish them well; they want everyone to wish their enemies ill.   HAROLD NICHOLSON

Ireland is a country in which the probable never happens and the
impossible always does.   JOHN PENTLAND MAHAFFY

Ireland is a fruitful mother of genius but a barren nurse.
                                       JOHN BOYLE O'REILLY

May the devil chase you every day of your life and never catch
you.   IRISH TOAST

When Irish eyes are smiling, watch your step.   GERALD KERSH

JEALOUSY

Jealousy is the dragon in paradise; the hell of heaven; and the most
bitter of the emotions because associated with the sweetest.
                                                  A. R. ORAGE

Jealousy would be far less torturous if we understood that love is a
passion entirely unrelated to our merits.   PAUL ELDRIDGE

The jealous are troublesome to others, but a torment to themselves.
                                                  WILLIAM PENN

It is not love that is blind but jealousy.   LAWRENCE DURRELL

It is enough for a man to have distinction and brains for every
common tongue to wag against him.   OSCAR WILDE

Jealousy does more harm than witchcraft.   GERMAN PROVERB

Anger and jealousy can no more bear to lose sight of their objects
than love.   GEORGE ELIOT

JEW

To be a Jew is a destiny.   VICKI BAUM

The Jews generally give value. They make you pay, but they deliver the goods.   GEORGE BERNARD SHAW

There is, of course, no greater fallacy than the one about the stingi-
ness of Jews. They are the most lavish and opulent race on earth.
                                                  THOMAS WOLFE

A Jewish man with parents alive is a fifteen-year-old boy, and will remain a fifteen-year-old boy till they die.   PHILIP ROTH

JOGGING AND RUNNING

Running through mud and rain is never boring. Like a hundred thousand cross-country runners, I find in running, win or lose, a deep satisfaction that I cannot express in any other way.

ROGER BANNISTER

Everything is prettier when you're running.   RICHARD STREBECH,
seventy-four years old

No jogger with any sense runs on a street that is polluted by gas fumes, except perhaps to get to and from where he does his jogging.   DR. DAVID M. MACDONALD

You need to take the initiative in a race. . . . The race usually goes to whoever's not afraid to commit himself.   BRENDAN FOSTER

If someone had offered me water in the Park, I would have stopped and had a drink and a chat. But no one did, so I pressed on.

BILL RODGERS,
after winning New York City Marathon

Running is relaxing. I can think out any problems I have more clearly when I'm running by myself.   JIM RYUN

Everyone who has run knows that its most important value is in removing tension and allowing a release from whatever other cares the day may bring.   JIMMY CARTER

If the poor overweight jogger only knew how far he had to run to work off the calories in a crust of bread he might find it better in terms of pound per mile to go to a massage parlor.

DR. CHRISTIAAN BARNARD

JOY

Without inequality there is no joy.   SAMUEL JOHNSON

Then there's the joy of getting your desk clean, and knowing that all your letters are answered, and you can see the wood on it again.

LADY BIRD JOHNSON

There is joy in the possibilities of any actual life, and a deeper joy that comes with a sense of sharing the whole and endless adventure of mankind.   IRWIN EDMAN

An element of abstention, of restraint, must enter into all finer joys.   VIDA D. SCUDDER

One joy scatters a hundred griefs.   CHINESE PROVERB

It is strange what a contempt men have for the joys that are offered them freely.   GEORGES DUHAMEL

This is the true joy in life, the being used for a purpose recognized by yourself as a mighty one.   GEORGE BERNARD SHAW

No human feeling can ever be so appalling as joy.   VICTOR HUGO

JUDGMENT

Don't judge anyone harshly until you yourself have been through his experiences.   GOETHE

The average man's judgment is so poor, he runs a risk every time he uses it.   E. W. HOWE

To judge wisely, we must know how things appear to the unwise.
                                            GEORGE ELIOT

The value and force of a man's judgment can be measured by his ability to think independently of his temperamental leanings.
                                       ALGERNON S. LOGAN

Make it a practice to judge persons and things in the most favorable light at all times and under all circumstances.
                                   SAINT VINCENT DE PAUL

In order to judge properly, one must get away somewhat from what one is judging, after having loved it. This is true of countries, of persons, and of oneself.   ANDRÉ GIDE

When responsibility is pressed heavily on anyone to make a judgment, it seems to me useful to have as close an understanding of the view of each side as possible.   JOHN F. KENNEDY

JUSTICE

It is possible to get justice done to others, never to oneself.

ALFRED CAPUS

Injustice is relatively easy to bear; it is justice that hurts.

H. L. MENCKEN

Corn can't expect justice from a court composed of chickens.

AFRICAN PROVERB

We will not be satisfied until justice rolls down like waters and righteousness like a mighty stream.   MARTIN LUTHER KING, JR.

No man suffers injustice without learning, vaguely but surely, what justice is.   ISAAC ROSENFELD

KINDNESS

One can pay back the loan of gold, but one dies forever in debt to those who are kind.   MALAYAN PROVERB

Be kind and considerate to others, depending somewhat upon who they are.   DON HEROLD

Kindness begets kindness.   SOPHOCLES

The milk of human kindness is less apt to turn sour if the vessel that holds it stands steady, cool, and separate, and is not too often uncorked.   GEORGE SANTAYANA

There is a kind way of assisting our fellow-creatures which is enough to break their hearts while it saves their outer envelope.

JOSEPH CONRAD

My feeling is that there is nothing in life but refraining from hurting others, and comforting those that are sad.   OLIVE SCHREINER

Nobody is kind only to one person at once, but to many persons in one.   FREDERICK W. FABER

KNOWLEDGE

To be master of any branch of knowledge, you must master those

which lie next to it; and thus to know anything you must know all.
OLIVER WENDELL HOLMES, JR.

If we would have new knowledge, we must get a whole world of new questions.
SUSANNE K. LANGER

Not to know is bad; not to wish to know is worse. AFRICAN PROVERB

No one sees further into a generalization than his own knowledge of details extends.
WILLIAM JAMES

If a little knowledge is dangerous, where is the man who has so much as to be out of danger?
THOMAS HENRY HUXLEY

The more one penetrates the realm of knowledge the more puzzling everything becomes.
HENRY MILLER

Strange how much you've got to know before you know how little you know.
ANONYMOUS

Knowledge rests not upon truth alone, but upon error also.
CARL G. JUNG

More and more, I used the quickness of my mind to pick the mind of other people and use their knowledge as my own.
ELEANOR ROOSEVELT

The struggling for knowledge has a pleasure in it like that of wrestling with a fine woman.
LORD HALIFAX

It is the tragedy of the world that no one knows what he doesn't know—and the less a man knows, the more sure he is that he knows everything.
JOYCE CARY

LANGUAGE

Slang is a language that rolls up its sleeves, spits on its hands, and goes to work.
CARL SANDBURG

It is so important for the purpose of thought to keep language efficient as it is in surgery to keep tetanus bacilli out of one's bandages.
EZRA POUND

The English language lacks a Continental air, but it is full of lovely dells and downs, mountains and lakes, a fine wholesome language.
GEORGE MOORE

Language is the most imperfect and expensive means yet discovered for communicating thought.   WILLIAM JAMES

My language is the common prostitute that I turn into a virgin.
KARL KRAUS

The limits of my language stand for the limits of my world.
LUDWIG WITTGENSTEIN

LATENESS

Punctuality is one of the cardinal virtues. Always insist on it in
your subordinates and dependents.   DON MARQUIS

If you're there before it's over, you're on time.   JAMES J. WALKER

He who is late may gnaw the bones.   YUGOSLAV PROVERB

In spite of all our speeding it's still the style to be late. KIN HUBBARD

LAUGHTER

We are able to laugh when we achieve detachment, if only for a
moment.   MAY SARTON

Laughter is the corrective force which prevents us from becoming
cranks.   HENRI BERGSON

If only men could be induced to laugh more they might hate less,
and find more serenity here on earth.   MALCOLM MUGGERIDGE

With the fearful strain that is on me night and day, if I did not
laugh I should die.   ABRAHAM LINCOLN

A sense of humor is what makes you laugh at something that
would make you mad if it happened to you.   ANONYMOUS

Men show their character in nothing more clearly than by what
they think laughable.   GOETHE

LAW AND LAWYERS

The houses of lawyers are roofed with the skins of litigants.
WELSH PROVERB

It is hard to say whether doctors of law or divinity have made the greater advances in the lucrative business of mystery.

EDMUND BURKE

A lawyer is a gentleman who rescues your estate from your enemies and keeps it for himself.   LORD BROUGHAM

It is the trade of lawyers to question everything, yield nothing, and talk by the hour.   HOLBROOK JACKSON

An appeal, Hennessy, is when you ask one court to show its contempt for another court.   FINLEY PETER DUNNE

Lawyers earn a living by the sweat of their browbeating.

JAMES G. HUNEKER

I am not so afraid of lawyers as I used to be. They are lambs in wolves' clothing.   EDNA ST. VINCENT MILLAY

One listens to one's lawyer prattle on as long as one can stand it and then signs where indicated.   ALEXANDER WOOLLCOTT

LEADERSHIP

A political leader is necessarily an impostor since he believes in solving life's problems without asking its question. ANDRÉ MALRAUX

Why do we need leaders in a free country? I would answer that the leader's function is to help determine, in any crisis, which of our possible selves will act.   LYMAN BRYSON

I suppose that leadership at one time meant muscle; but today it means getting along with people.   INDIRA GANDHI

I am certainly not one of those who need to be prodded. In fact, if anything, I am the prod.   SIR WINSTON CHURCHILL

If you doubt you can accomplish something, then you can't accomplish it. You have to have confidence in your ability, and then be tough enough to follow through.   ROSALYNN CARTER,
on being asked what qualities make a leader

Good fellows are a dime a dozen, but an aggressive leader is priceless.   RED BLAIK

A leader or a man of action in a crisis almost always acts subconsciously and then thinks of the reasons for his action.

JAWAHARLAL NEHRU

Charlatanism of some degree is indispensable to effective leadership.   ERIC HOFFER

De Gaulle did not call in "writers"; the very idea is grotesque. The leader who allows others to speak for him is abdicating.

MAY SARTON

To be a leader of men one must turn one's back on men.

HAVELOCK ELLIS

In the case of political, and even of religious, leaders it is often very doubtful whether they have done more good or harm.

ALBERT EINSTEIN

LEARNING

No man deeply engaged in serious work has time to learn.

JOSEPH HERGESHEIMER

Once learning solidifies, all is over with it.

ALFRED NORTH WHITEHEAD

Learning is not easy, but hard; culture is severe. The steps to Parnassus are steep and terribly arduous.   JOHN JAY CHAPMAN

The man who is too old to learn was probably always too old to learn.   HENRY S. HASKINS

Whoever cares to learn will always find a teacher. GERMAN PROVERB

There are no easy methods of learning difficult things; the method is to close your door, give out that you are not at home, and work.

JOSEPH DE MAISTRE

There are many things which we can afford to forget which it is yet well to learn.   OLIVER WENDELL HOLMES, JR.

LEISURE

There is precious little hope to be got out of whatever keeps us industrious, but there is a chance for us whenever we cease work and become stargazers.   H. M. TOMLINSON

Leisure only means a chance to do other jobs that demand attention.   OLIVER WENDELL HOLMES, JR.

The real problem of your leisure is how to keep other people from using it.   ANONYMOUS

It is impossible to enjoy idling thoroughly, unless one has plenty of work to do.   JEROME K. JEROME

Leisure is the curse of the poor in spirit.   NORMAN DOUGLAS

It is in his pleasure that a man really lives; it is from his leisure that he constructs the true fabric of self.   AGNES REPPLIER

LETTERS

Dear Mrs. Jones:
    Thank you for your letter. I shall try to do better.
                                                   CARL SANDBURG,
                                       form letter used for replying
                                                to critical letters

In an age like ours, which is not given to letter-writing, we forget what an important part it used to play in people's lives.
                                                   ANATOLE BROYARD

One man was so mad at me that he ended his letter: "Beware. . . . You will never get out of this world alive."   JOHN STEINBECK

The one good thing about not seeing you is that I can write you letters.   SVETLANA ALLILUYEVA

I consider it a good rule for letter-writing to leave unmentioned what the recipient already knows, and instead tell him something new.   SIGMUND FREUD

It takes two to write a letter as much as it takes two to make a quarrel.   ELIZABETH DREW

LIFE

Life is so largely controlled by chance that its conduct can be but a perpetual improvisation.   W. SOMERSET MAUGHAM

There is one word which may serve as a rule of practice for all one's life—reciprocity.   CONFUCIUS

If all human lives depended upon their usefulness—as might be judged by certain standards—there would be a sudden and terrific mortality in the world.   GENE TUNNEY

Life will always remain a gamble, with prizes sometimes for the imprudent, and blanks so often to the wise.   JEROME K. JEROME

For if there is a sin against life, it consists perhaps not so much in despairing of life as in hoping for another life and in eluding the implacable grandeur of this life.   ALBERT CAMUS

Life is easier than you'd think; all that is necessary is to accept the impossible, do without the indispensable, and bear the intolerable.

KATHLEEN NORRIS

Fear not that life shall come to an end, but rather fear that it shall never have a beginning.   JOHN HENRY CARDINAL NEWMAN

If life were predictable, it would cease to be life and be without flavor.   ELEANOR ROOSEVELT

The tragedy of life is not so much what men suffer, but rather what they miss.   THOMAS CARLYLE

There is more to life than increasing its speed. MOHANDAS K. GANDHI

There is a strange reluctance on the part of most people to admit that they enjoy life.   WILLIAM LYON PHELPS

The first half of our lives is ruined by our parents and the second half by our children.   CLARENCE DARROW

Life is made up of constant calls to action, and we seldom have time for more than hastily contrived answers.   LEARNED HAND

Life is not having been told that the man has just waxed the floor.

OGDEN NASH

What is life? It is the flash of a firefly in the night.   CROWFOOT,
of the Blackfeet

Life is little more than a loan shark: It exacts a very high rate of interest for the few pleasures it concedes.   LUIGI PIRANDELLO

A great part of life consists in contemplating what we cannot cure.

ROBERT LOUIS STEVENSON

I don't believe medical discoveries are doing much to advance human life. As fast as we create ways to extend it we are inventing ways to shorten it.   DR. CHRISTIAAN BARNARD

If you stop struggling, then you stop life.   HUEY NEWTON

Life is what we make it, always has been, always will be.

GRANDMA MOSES

To live remains an art which everyone must learn, and which no one can teach.   HAVELOCK ELLIS

Serenity of spirit and turbulence of action should make up the sum of a man's life.   VITA SACKVILLE-WEST

It is while you are patiently toiling at the little tasks of life that the meaning and shape of the great whole of life dawn on you.

PHILLIPS BROOKS

The great use of life is to spend it for something that outlasts it.

WILLIAM JAMES

To live is like to love—all reason is against it, and all healthy instinct for it.   SAMUEL BUTLER

LISTENING

You can't fake listening. It shows.   RAQUEL WELCH

Lenin could listen so intently that he exhausted the speaker.

SIR ISAIAH BERLIN

One of the best ways to persuade others is with your ears—by listening to them.   DEAN RUSK

While the right to talk may be the beginning of freedom, the necessity of listening is what makes that right important.

WALTER LIPPMANN

He understands badly who listens badly.   WELSH PROVERB

When people talk, listen completely. Most people never listen.

ERNEST HEMINGWAY

From listening comes wisdom, and from speaking repentance.

ITALIAN PROVERB

A man is already halfway in love with a woman who listens to him.

BRENDAN FRANCIS

People will listen a great deal more patiently while you explain your mistakes than when you explain your successes.

WILBUR N. NESBIT

LITERATURE

The critics will say as always that literature is decaying. From the time of the first critic up to now they have said nothing else.

SIR OSBERT SITWELL

The test of real literature is that it will bear repetition. We read over the same pages again and again, and always with fresh delight. SAMUAL MC CHORD CROTHERS

Society must be saved in literature as well as in politics.

VICTOR HUGO

I doubt if anything learnt at school is of more value than great literature learnt by heart. SIR RICHARD LIVINGSTONE

The duty of literature is to note what counts, and to light up what is suited to the light. If it ceases to choose and to love, it becomes like a woman who gives herself without preference.

ANATOLE FRANCE

LONELINESS

Loneliness and the feeling of being unwanted are the most terrible poverty. MOTHER TERESA OF CALCUTTA

We must always be more or less lonely, but sometimes it is given to spirit to touch spirit. . . . Then we understand and are understood.

JANET ERSKINE STUART

Bad as I like ye, it's worse without ye. IRISH PROVERB

Men love because they are afraid of themselves, afraid of the loneliness that lives in them, and need someone in whom they can lose themselves as smoke loses itself in the sky. V. F. CALVERTON

Loneliness can be conquered only by those who can bear solitude.

PAUL TILLICH

If you are afraid of loneliness, don't marry. ANTON CHEKOV

LOVE

If you must love your neighbor as yourself, it is at least as fair to love yourself as your neighbor. NICHOLAS DE CHAMFORT

The best practical advice I can give to the present generation is to practice the virtue which the Christians call love.

BERTRAND RUSSELL

Love is the active concern for the life and growth of that which we love.   ERICH FROMM

Love does not care to define and is never in a hurry to do so.

CHARLES DU BOS

Love does not express itself on command; it cannot be called out like a dog to its master—merely because one thinks he needs to see it. Love is autonomous; it obeys only itself.   ROBERT C. MURPHY

No word is used with more meanings than this term, most of the meanings being dishonest in that they cover up the real underlying motives in the relationship.   ROLLO MAY

A person who is unable to love cannot reveal himself.

HELEN MERRELL LYND

The best thing we can do for those we love is to help them escape from us.   BARON FRIEDRICH VON HUGEL

True love is a discipline in which each divines the secret self of the other and refuses to believe in the mere daily self.

WILLIAM BUTLER YEATS

We can only love what we know and we can never know completely what we do not love.   ALDOUS HUXLEY

It is not often for merit that people are loved.   C. E. MONTAGUE

Love in action is a harsh and dreadful thing compared with love in dreams.   FYODOR DOSTOEVSKI

LOVE: MAN AND WOMAN

A man can be happy with any woman as long as he does not love her.   OSCAR WILDE

Woman begins by resisting a man's advances and ends by blocking his retreat.   OSCAR WILDE

Love is the greatest refreshment in life.   PABLO PICASSO

Love, love, love—all the wretched cant of it, masking egotism, lust,

masochism, fantasy under a mythology of sentimental postures.
GERMAINE GREER

A woman should soften but not weaken a man.   SIGMUND FREUD

Love . . . is mutuality of devotion forever subduing the antagonisms inherent in divided functions.   ERIK ERIKSON

Young men still desire women as much as ever, even though they don't want to marry them as much.   CLARE BOOTH LUCE

Love does not begin and end the way we seem to think it does. Love is a battle, love is a war; love is a growing up. JAMES BALDWIN

An old man in love is like a flower in winter. PORTUGUESE PROVERB

There are women who do not like to cause suffering to many men at a time, and who prefer to concentrate on one man: These are the faithful women.   ALFRED CAPUS

The love game is never called off on account of darkness.
TOM MASSON

A lover is a man who tries to be more amiable than it is possible for him to be.   NICHOLAS DE CHAMFORT

No partner in a love relationship (whether homosexual or heterosexual) should feel that he has to give up an essential part of himself to make it viable.   MAY SARTON

One of my theories is that men love with their eyes; women love with their ears.   ZSA ZSA GABOR

Love is a thing that sharpens all our wits.   ITALIAN PROVERB

If you wish women to love you, be original; I know a man who used to wear fur hats summer and winter, and women fell in love with him.   ANTON CHEKOV

I was in love with a beautiful blonde once—she drove me to drink— 'tis the one thing I'm indebted to her for.   W. C. FIELDS

What "love" is I don't know if it is not the response of our deepest natures to one another.   WILLIAM CARLOS WILLIAMS

Seek not the favor of women. So shall you find it, indeed.
RUDYARD KIPLING

I do not spoil women . . . I don't send them flowers and gifts . . . I am saving those gestures until I am an unpleasant old man who must resort to bribery to win a woman's synthetic affections.

GEORGE SANDERS

Nobody will ever win the Battle of the Sexes. There's just too much fraternizing with the enemy.   HENRY KISSINGER

Love is like those second-rate hotels where all the luxury is the lobby.   PAUL-JEAN TOULET

A woman who loves her husband is merely paying her bills. A woman who loves her lover gives alms to the poor.

PAUL-JEAN TOULET

A man is so important for a woman; he changes her life.

SOPHIA LOREN

Never pretend to a love which you do not actually feel, for love is not ours to command.   ALAN WATTS

A woman never forgets the men she could have had; a man, the women he couldn't.   AUGUSTA DOCKERY

The story of a love is not important—what is important is that one is capable of love. It is perhaps the only glimpse we are permitted of eternity.   HELEN HAYES

He felt now that he was not simply close to her, but that he did not know where he ended and she began.   LEO TOLSTOY

Love is like a bazaar. The admittance is free but it costs you something before you get out.   SYDNEY TREMAYNE

I like not only to be loved, but to be told I am loved. GEORGE ELIOT

LUCK

The world is inescapably shot through with luck, because it is also shot through with freedom.   JOYCE CARY

Luck is the residue of design.   BRANCH RICKEY

Luck sometimes visits a fool, but never sits down with him.

GERMAN PROVERB

People who believe they're going to have good luck and find the answer usually do find it because they've put the idea of their success into their subconscious.   BILL LEAR

Luck, bad if not good, will always be with us. But it has a way of favoring the intelligent and showing its back to the stupid.

JOHN DEWEY

It would seem that you don't be having any good luck until you believe there is no such thing as luck in it at all.   IRISH PROVERB

The only sure thing about luck is that it will change.   BRET HARTE

MAN (HUMANITY)

Man is an intelligence in servitude to his organs.   ALDOUS HUXLEY

Man is the missing link between the ape and the human being.

ANONYMOUS

Man will become better only when you will make him see what he is like.   ANTON CHEKOV

Man uses his intelligence less in the care of his own species than he does in his care of anything else he owns or governs.

DR. ABRAHAM MEYERSON

Man is harder than rock and more fragile than an egg.

YUGOSLAV PROVERB

We get lost in a fog of abstractions and easily forget that man is a bloodhound sniffing out the real.   ROBERT C. POLLOCK

The great human asset is man himself.   ANATOLE FRANCE

Men are very queer animals—a mixture of horse-nervousness, ass-stubbornness and camel-malice.   THOMAS HENRY HUXLEY

Whenever there is lost the consciousness that every man is an object of concern for us just because he is a man, civilization and morals are shaken, and the advance to fully developed inhumanity is only a question of time.   ALBERT SCHWEITZER

MAN (MALE)

Men are a sort of animal, that if ever they are constant, it is only when they are ill-used.   LADY MARY WORTLEY MONTAGU

My theory is that men are no more liberated than women.

INDIRA GANDHI

Some men have a den in their home, while others just growl all over the house.   ANONYMOUS

Don't tell a man he's a saint; he knows better. Tell him he's a devil; he'll believe it and be flattered.   F. M. KNOWLES

Men have more problems than women. In the first place, they have to put up with women.   FRANÇOISE SAGAN

Men hate to be misunderstood, and to be understood makes them furious.   EDGAR SALTUS

There is nothing will kill a man so soon as having nobody to find fault with but himself.   GEORGE ELIOT

When they are cooking . . . they won't let anyone near them. But if a woman is preparing a meal, try to keep them out of the kitchen.

LUCILLE BALL

Men love putting women on a pedestal because it's so much more satisfying when they knock them off. They fall farther.

CLARE BOOTH LUCE

Men are always ready to respect anything that bores them.

MARILYN MONROE

Several men I can think of are as capable, as smart, as funny, as compassionate, and as confused—as remarkable you might say—as most women.   JANE HOWARD

Why will a man say, "No sense in calling an electrician—I can fix that"—and we spend the rest of the evening in total darkness?

GYPSY ROSE LEE

Men err when they think they can be inhuman exploiters in their business life, and loving husbands and fathers at home.

DR. SMILEY BLANTON

Not only it is harder to be a man, it is also harder to become one.

ARIANNA STASSINOPOULOS

Women declare they honor a good man, but given their choice, most of them would select one a little speckled.   MINNA T. ANTRIM

Men imagine that a woman has no individual existence, and that she ought always to be absorbed in them.   GEORGE SAND

MARRIAGE

The chief reason why marriage is rarely a success is that it is contracted while the partners are insane.   DR. JOSEPH COLLINS

It is not marriage that fails; it is people that fail. All that marriage does is to show people up.   HARRY EMERSON FOSDICK

Marriage is one of the few ceremonies left to us about which it is impossible—or at least self-demeaning—to be cynical. Then, in secret, be joyful.   JOHN LEONARD

Originally marriage meant the sale of a woman by one man to another; now most women sell themselves though they have no intention of delivering the goods listed in the bill of sale.

ROBERT GRAVES

A certain sort of talent is indispensable for people who would spend years together and not bore themselves to death.

ROBERT LOUIS STEVENSON

Marriage has teeth, and him bite very hot.   JAMAICAN PROVERB

A fellow ought to save a few of the long evenings he spends with his girl till after they're married.   KIN HUBBARD

Wedlock: The deep, deep peace of the double bed after the hurly-burly of the chaise longue.   MRS. PATRICK CAMPBELL

Women do generally manage to love the guys they marry. They manage to love the guy they marry more than they manage to marry the guy they love.   CLARE BOOTH LUCE

The chain of wedlock is so heavy that it takes two to carry it—sometimes three.   ALEXANDRE DUMAS

More marriages have been ruined by irritating habits than by unfaithfulness.   H. R. L. SHEPPARD

It isn't tying himself to one woman that a man dreads when he thinks of marrying, it's separating himself from all the others.

HELEN ROWLAND

When love became devotion instead of possession, marriage reached the climax of its slow ascent from brutality. WILL DURANT

I don't think it would be a bad idea if we dissolved the whole idea of marriage. I think possibly we'd end up doing the same things we're doing now anyway.   BURT REYNOLDS

Every woman must admit, and every man with as much sense as a woman, that it's very hard to make a home for any man if he's always in it. WINIFRED KIRKLAND

As bad as marrying the devil's daughter and living with the old folks. ENGLISH PROVERB

Marriage always demands the greatest understanding of the art of insincerity possible between two human beings. VICKI BAUM

Never go to bed mad. Stay up and fight. PHYLLIS DILLER

I generally had to give in. NAPOLEON BONAPARTE, *speaking of his relations with Empress Josephine*

Marriage . . . begins, not with setting up house, counting wedding presents, blowing kisses, looking at wedding groups, but with two bodies confronting one another like two wrestlers. MALCOLM MUGGERIDGE

It destroys one's nerves to be amiable every day to the same human being. BENJAMIN DISRAELI

Never get married in the morning, because you never know who you'll meet that night. PAUL HORNUNG

MEMORY

If we remembered everything, we should on most occasions be as badly off as if we remembered nothing. WILLIAM JAMES

From the subterranean ore of memory we extract the jeweled visions of our future. MIGUEL DE UNAMUNO

Memory is a crazy woman that hoards colored rags and throws away food. AUSTIN O'MALLEY

Everybody needs his memories. They keep the wolf of insignificance from the door. SAUL BELLOW

Memory is not just the imprint of the past time upon us; it is the keeper of what is meaningful for our deepest hopes and fears. ROLLO MAY

Some memories are realities, and are better than anything that can ever happen to one again.   WILLA CATHER

The existence of forgetting has never been proved: We only know that some things don't come to mind when we want them.

FRIEDRICH NIETZSCHE

A great memory is never made synonymous with wisdom, any more than a dictionary would be called a treatise.

JOHN HENRY CARDINAL NEWMAN

MIND

It is discouraging to try to penetrate a mind like yours. You ought to get it out and dance on it. That would take some of the rigidity out of it.   MARK TWAIN

We should not only use the brains we have, but all that we can borrow.   WOODROW WILSON

There is no instrument so deceptive as the mind.   ST. JOHN ERVINE

He has a first-rate mind until he makes it up.

LADY VIOLET BONHAM CARTER

Few minds wear out; more rust out.   CHRISTIAN N. BOVEE

When I was a boy, they used to say that "only a mule and a milepost never changed its mind."   BERNARD M. BARUCH

A mind that is safe, secure, is a bourgeois mind, a shoddy mind. Yet that is what all of us want: to be completely safe.

J. KRISHNAMURTI

No mind, however loving, could bear to see plainly into all the recesses of another mind.   ARNOLD BENNETT

Might we not say to the confused voices which sometimes arise from the depths of our being: "Ladies, be so kind as to speak only four at a time"?   MADAME SWETCHINE

Nothing in life is as good as the marriage of true minds between man and woman. As good? It is life itself.   PEARL BUCK

The mind is the most capricious of insects—flitting, fluttering.

VIRGINIA WOOLF

MIRACLE

Miracles happen only to those who believe in them.

FRENCH PROVERB

The highest part of the art of life is the expectation of miracles.

WILLIAM BOLITHO

The world believes in the wonder worker, not in the words of wisdom.

RICHARD JEFFERIES

After all, I don't see why I am always asking for private, individual, selfish miracles when every year there are miracles like white dogwood.

ANNE MORROW LINDBERGH

Every man expects some miracle—either from his mind or from his body or from someone else or from events.

PAUL VALÉRY

Existence in itself, taken at its least miraculous, is a miracle.

REBECCA WEST

MISTAKE

There are few, very few, that will own themselves in a mistake, though all the world see them to be in downright nonsense.

JONATHAN SWIFT

All the mistakes I make arise from forsaking my own station and trying to see the object from another person's point of view.

RALPH WALDO EMERSON

Our blunders mostly come from letting our wishes interpret our duties.

ANONYMOUS

There is nothing final about a mistake, except its being taken as final.

PHYLLIS BOTTOME

It is very easy to forgive others their mistakes; it takes more grit to forgive them for having witnessed your own.

JESSAMYN WEST

Only he who does nothing makes a mistake.

FRENCH PROVERB

One cannot too soon forget his errors and misdemeanors; for to dwell upon them is to add to the offense.

HENRY DAVID THOREAU

Mistakes fail in their mission of helping the person who blames them on the other fellow.

HENRY S. HASKINS

The Providence that watches over the affairs of men works out their mistakes, at times, to a healthier issue than could have been accomplished by their wisest forethought.   JAMES A. FROUDE

MODEL

No girl in her right mind should deliberately set out to become a model.   JOHN ROBERT POWERS

You have to have the kind of body that doesn't need a girdle in order to get to pose in one.   CAROLYN KENMORE

When crack photographers and great producers want to use you again and again, it means you've got it. No amount of bed hopping or crotch politics is any substitute. You've either got it or you haven't.   CAROLYN KENMORE

Heaven knows there are few more interesting occupations today for an attractive girl.   CANDY JONES

It must be hard to be a model, because you'd want to be like the photograph of you, and you can't ever look that way.

ANDY WARHOL

There's a whole new legion of Brooke Shields clones coming along. Everyone was tired of the contrived look, and they started using young girls because they looked fresh.   JOHN PEDEN,
fashion photographer

I think there is a certain monotony about the girls of today. It must be planned that way.   DIANA VREELAND

MODERN AGE

There is an enormous amount of goodness and goodwill and right feeling and action in the modern world.   SIR RICHARD LIVINGSTONE

The modern world belongs to the half-educated, a rather difficult class, because they do not realize how little they know.

WILLIAM R. INGE

The private lives of the ancients are now the public sport of the moderns.   IVOR BROWN

It is hardly respectable to be good nowadays.   EDITH SITWELL

This is perhaps the most beautiful time in human history; it is really pregnant with all kinds of creative possibilities made possible by science and technology which now constitute the slave of man—if man is not enslaved by it.   JONAS SALK

I do not fear computers. I fear the lack of them.   ISAAC ASIMOV

The age is a vociferous one, and no prophet is without honor who is able to strike an attitude and to speak loud enough to make himself heard.   ELLEN GLASGOW

If it keeps up, man will atrophy all his limbs but the push-button finger.   FRANK LLOYD WRIGHT

I sometimes think of what future historians will say of us. A single sentence will suffice for modern man: He fornicated and read the papers.   ALBERT CAMUS

Our age will be known as the age of committees.   SIR ERNEST BENN

Ours is an excessively conscious age. We *know* so much, we feel so little.   D. H. LAWRENCE

Perhaps this is an age when men think bravely of the human spirit; for surely they have a strange lust to lay it bare.

CHRISTOPHER MORLEY

The present age, for all its cosmopolitan hustle, is curiously suburban in spirit.   NORMAN DOUGLAS

MOMENT

It may be life is only worthwhile at moments. Perhaps that is all we ought to expect.   SHERWOOD ANDERSON

The living moment is everything.   D. H. LAWRENCE

I recognize that I live now and only now, and I will do what I want to do *this* moment and not what I decided was best for me yesterday.   HUGH PRATHER

Single moments, improved or wasted, are the salvation or ruin of all-important interests.   JOHN HENRY CARDINAL NEWMAN

If you let yourself be absorbed completely, if you surrender completely to the moments as they pass, you live more richly those moments.   ANNE MORROW LINDBERGH

Seize from every moment its unique novelty and do not prepare your joys.   ANDRÉ GIDE

MONEY

It frees you from doing things you dislike. Since I dislike doing nearly everything, money is handy.   GROUCHO MARX

If women didn't exist, all the money in the world would have no meaning.   ARISTOTLE ONASSIS

Those who believe money can do everything are frequently prepared to do everything for money.   ANONYMOUS

The greatest waste of money is to keep it.   JACKIE GLEASON

Those who help us make money seldom lose all our esteem.

J. PETIT-SENN

I know of nothing which gives a man a greater feeling of well-being than when he has touched a fellow for a tenner and got away with it.   EDGAR WALLACE

Million dollars: A sum that may be honestly acquired by putting aside five hundred dollars out of one's salary every week for forty years.   ANONYMOUS

Who recalls when folks got along without something if it cost too much?   KIN HUBBARD

Making money is easy; knowing what to do with it becomes a problem.   RING LARDNER

There is no economy in going to bed early to save candles if the results be twins.   CHINESE PROVERB

Oh, I wish I were a miser; being a miser is so occupying.

GERTRUDE STEIN

My father was never particularly interested in making money. And neither am I. He always said that if you do the right thing, and build your bridges strong, it will come automatically.

PHILIP K. WRIGLEY

Money doesn't buy happiness. It buys great hookers—but not happiness.   BURT REYNOLDS

I've always felt that if you could develop an answer to a need, this was the way to make money. Most people are more anxious to make money than they are to find a need. And without the need, you're working uphill.   BILL LEAR

Money is necessary—both to support a family and to advance causes one believes in.   CORETTA SCOTT KING

Money is round. It rolls away.   SHOLEM ALEICHEM

It is a kind of spiritual snobbery that makes people think they can be happy without money.   ALBERT CAMUS

I am not quite sure what the advantage is in having a few more dollars to spend if the air is too dirty to breathe, the water too polluted to drink, the commuters are losing out in the struggle to get in and out of the city, the streets are filthy, and the schools so bad that the young perhaps wisely stay away, and the hoodlums roll citizens for some of the dollars they saved in the tax cut.

JOHN KENNETH GALBRAITH

Everything in the world may be endured except continual prosperity.   GOETHE

MORALITY

We are doomed to be moral and cannot help ourselves.

JOHN HAYNES HOLMES

We have two kinds of morality side by side: one which we preach but do not practice and another which we practice but seldom preach.   BERTRAND RUSSELL

Our morality seems to be only a check on the ultimate domination of force, just as our politeness is a check on the impulse of every pig to put his feet in the trough.   OLIVER WENDELL HOLMES, JR.

Anglo-Saxon morality . . . takes such very good care that its prophecies of woe to the erring person shall find fulfillment.

GEORGE GISSING

You can never tell the sinner from the Christian. They drink the same drinks and smoke the same cigars.

AIMEE SEMPLE MC PHERSON

Morality may consist solely in the courage of making a choice.

LÉON BLUM

Moral indignation is jealousy with a halo. H. G. WELLS

The world of empirical morality consists for the most part of nothing but ill will and envy. GOETHE

It would be possible to argue that a good sheep dog has attained almost the summit of moral excellence. WILLIAM R. INGE

I've met so many people, often the scum of the earth, and found them, you know, quite decent. I am an uncomfortable stranger to moral indignation. W. SOMERSET MAUGHAM

Moral education is impossible apart from the habitual vision of greatness. ALFRED NORTH WHITEHEAD

MOTHER

A suburban mother's role is to deliver children obstetrically once, and by car forever after. PETER DE VRIES

I never had a mother. I suppose a mother is one to whom you hurry when you are troubled. EMILY DICKINSON

My mother was dead for five years before I knew that I had loved her very much. LILLIAN HELLMAN

The mother who spoils her child fattens a serpent. SPANISH PROVERB

A mother never gets hit with a custard pie . . . never. MACK SENNETT

The torment that so many young women know, bound hand and foot by love and motherhood, without having forgotten their former dreams. SIMONE DE BEAUVOIR

Women are aristocrats, and it is always the mother who makes us feel that we belong to the better sort. JOHN LANCASTER SPALDING

The mother cult is something that will set future generations roaring with laughter. GUSTAVE FLAUBERT

Now, as always, the most automated appliance in a household is the mother. BEVERLY JONES

MOVIES

A real star has to have a motor, something hurrying underneath the hood.   DORE SCHARY

In case of an air raid, go directly to RKO—they haven't had a hit in years.   ANONYMOUS WIT,
1942

Most horror movies are certainly that.   BRENDAN FRANCIS

Everybody kisses everybody else in this crummy business all the time. It's the kissiest business in the world.   AVA GARDNER

Hollywood is a place where people from Iowa mistake each other for stars.   FRED ALLEN

The movie world is full of pathetic flops and has-beens, with no hope of making a comeback, and because we know that a flop lurks inside of every one of us, the anguish is there, day and night, film after film.   SOPHIA LOREN

Too caustic? To hell with the cost, we'll make the picture anyway.
SAMUEL GOLDWYN

A man can make more money with less effort in the movies than in any other profession.   GEORGE SANDERS

Some films are slices of life, mine are slices of cake.
ALFRED HITCHCOCK

Movies are the art form most like man's imagination.
FRANCIS FORD COPPOLA

What do you see now when you go to the movies? A terrified girl being raped by four or five idiots on a beach. They make burlesque look like *Rebecca of Sunnybrook Farm*.   ANN CORIO

A rock's a rock, a tree is a tree, shoot it in bed. HOLLYWOOD SAYING

What puzzles most of us are the things which have been left in the movies rather than the things which have been taken out.
AGNES REPPLIER

MUSIC

The joy of music should never be interrupted by a commercial.
LEONARD BERNSTEIN

Rock music in its lyrics often talks ahead of the time about what's going on in the country. EDMUND G. BROWN

Men profess to be lovers of music, but for the most part they give no evidence in their opinions and lives that they have heard it. HENRY DAVID THOREAU

What is the Ninth Symphony compared to a pop tune played by a hurdy-gurdy and a memory! KARL KRAUS

A splendid brass band has just been playing a few pieces on the street, in the rain. It felt like velvet to one's inner being. HENRI FREDERIC AMIEL

Good music isn't nearly so bad as it sounds. HARRY ZELZER, *Chicago impresario*

Nobody dreams of music in hell, and nobody conceives of heaven without it. S. PARKES CADMAN

Music alone has the power to make us penetrate into ourselves; the other arts offer us only eccentric pleasures. HONORÉ DE BALZAC

Music is the only language in which you cannot say a mean or sarcastic thing. JOHN ERSKINE

Classical music is the kind that we keep hopin' will turn into a tune. KIN HUBBARD

Music expresses that which cannot be said and on which it is impossible to be silent. VICTOR HUGO

A very great part of the pleasure people take in music comes from the associations it revives. LELAND HALL

NATURE

The old Lakota was wise. He knew that man's heart away from nature becomes hard; he knew that lack of respect for growing, living things soon led to lack of respect for humans too. CHIEF LUTHER STANDING BEAR

Nature reserves the right to inflict upon her children the most terrifying jests. THORNTON WILDER

The sacredness of things—could not spit on a stream without a sense of desecration. RICHARD JEFFERIES

Nature takes away any faculty that is not used.   WILLIAM R. INGE

Politics—I don't know why, but they seem to have a tendency to separate us, to keep us from one another, while nature is always and ever making efforts to bring us together.   SEAN O'CASEY

No creature is fully itself till it is, like the dandelion, opened in the bloom of pure relationship to the sun, the entire living cosmos.

D. H. LAWRENCE

NEIGHBOR

How seldom we weigh our neighbors in the same balance as ourselves.   THOMAS À KEMPIS

This, I think, is our task today: to learn to combine the command to love our neighbors as ourselves with finding out who our neighbors are and knowing all that there is to know about them.

MARGARET MEAD

No one can afford to let his neighbors know what he is thinking about them.   LIN YUTANG

No one is rich enough to do without a neighbor.   DANISH PROVERB

While the spirit of neighborliness was important on the frontier because neighbors were so few, it is even more important now because our neighbors are so many.   LADY BIRD JOHNSON

Love thy neighbor, but pull not down thy hedge.   JOHN RAY

If you want to hear the whole truth about yourself, anger your neighbor.   ANONYMOUS

Bread for myself is a material question. Bread for my neighbor is a spiritual one.   NICHOLAS BERDYAEV

NEWSPAPER

A breakfast without a newspaper is a horse without a saddle.

WILL ROGERS

Harmony seldom makes a headline.   SILAS BENT

If you don't have this freedom of the press, then all these little fellows are weaseling around and doing their monkey business and they never get caught. JUDGE HAROLD R. MEDINA

This is a dull life, and the only excuse for the existence of newspapers is that they should make it less dull. PETER FLEMING

Journalism—a profession whose business it is to explain to others what it personally does not understand. LORD NORTHCLIFFE

A good newspaper, I suppose, is a nation talking to itself.

ARTHUR MILLER

NEW YORK

How often, at difficult moments, I looked to New York, I listened to New York, to find out what you were thinking and feeling here, and always I found a comforting echo. CHARLES DE GAULLE

New York has a trip-hammer vitality which drives you insane with restlessness if you have no inner stabilizer. HENRY MILLER

In New York, a citizen is likely to keep on the move, shopping for the perfect arrangement of rooms and vistas, changing his habitation according to fortune, whim, and need. E. B. WHITE

New Yorkers are nice about giving you street directions; in fact, they seem quite proud of knowing where they are themselves.

KATHARINE BRUSH

If there were one city I should pick to live in, it would be New York. It is a city where I walk down the street and feel anything is possible. MARIA SCHELL

You know, the more they knock New York, the bigger it gets.

WILL ROGERS

New York is the only real city-city. TRUMAN CAPOTE

NOISE

An inability to stay quiet is one of the most conspicuous failings of mankind. WALTER BAGEHOT

Nowadays most men lead lives of noisy desperation.

JAMES THURBER

Noise, crowding, pollution, and the sheer rush of our complex, modern society are rapidly becoming as oppressive to many individuals as the worst kind of political dictatorship.

THOMAS F. EAGLETON

Noise is evolving not only the endurers of noise but the needers of noise.   EDWIN WAY TEALE

He who sleeps in continual noise is awakened by silence.

WILLIAM DEAN HOWELLS

Everybody has their taste in noises as well as in other matters.

JANE AUSTEN

NUDITY

Nude scenes are made for audiences; it is most boring for a director.   HENRI-GEORGE CLOUZOT

I don't know why I'm here. I'm only nude because there's nothing to do here with your clothes on.   CLIENT AT A SWINGERS' CLUB,
Time

Why should I care what part of my body I reveal. . . . Is not all body and soul an instrument through which the artist expresses his inner message of beauty?   ISADORA DUNCAN

Gable the King could leer at you in a movie and it was ten times more sexy than a whole soundstage of nudes.   JOAN CRAWFORD

Beauty in the flesh will continue to rule the world.

FLORENZ ZIEGFELD

A reporter who visited a nudist camp asked one of the campers, "How did you get to be a nudist?" The camper replied, "I was born that way."   LEONARD LYONS

A thousand men can't undress a naked man.   GREEK PROVERB

No beauty she doth miss
When all her robes are on:
But beauty's self is she
When all her robes are gone.

ANONYMOUS,
madrigal, 1602

A woman is truly beautiful only when she is naked and she knows it.   ANDRÉ COURREGES

If it was the fashion to go naked, the face would be hardly observed.   LADY MARY WORTLEY MONTAGU

Man is the sole animal whose nudity offends his own companions, and the only one who, in his natural actions, withdraws and hides himself from his own kind.   MONTAIGNE

Nudist camps: Started by a group of sunbathers who, in their search for a perfect tan, were determined to leave no stern untoned.   CHARLES DWELLEY

For a woman to be loved, she usually ought to be naked.
                                                                          PIERRE CARDIN

A young woman who hasn't posed in the nude can barely lay claim to having been photographed.   BRENDAN FRANCIS

We had nudity on the stage in my youth . . . in the Ziegfeld Follies. But it was beautiful nudity. Now, it's sort of grubby. HELEN HAYES

In literature as in the plastic arts and in life itself, the nude is nearer to virtue than the *décolleté*.   HAVELOCK ELLIS

There come moods when these clothes of ours are not only too irksome to wear, but are themselves indecent.   WALT WHITMAN

If bodies please thee, praise God on occasion of them, and turn back thy love upon their maker.   SAINT AUGUSTINE

OPINION

If three people say you are an ass, put on a bridle. SPANISH PROVERB

When some folks agree with my opinions I begin to suspect I'm wrong.   KIN HUBBARD

The man who never alters his opinion is like standing water, and breeds reptiles of the mind.   WILLIAM BLAKE

Loyalty to a petrified opinion never yet broke a chain or freed a human soul.   MARK TWAIN

Opinion is that exercise of the human will which helps us to make a decision without information.   JOHN ERSKINE

Lidian says that the only sin which people never forgive in each other is a difference of opinion.   RALPH WALDO EMERSON

But it is just when opinions universally prevail and we have added lip service to their authority that we become sometimes most keenly conscious that we do not believe a word that we are saying.

VIRGINIA WOOLF

In all matters of opinion our adversaries are insane.   MARK TWAIN

I speak my opinion freely of all things, even of those that, perhaps, exceed my capacity.   MONTAIGNE

The best security for fixedness of opinion is, that people should be incapable of comprehending what is to be said on the other side.

WALTER BAGEHOT

OPPORTUNITY

I'm not the kind of a guy to knock at a door and then when the door is opened not go in.   WILLIAM SAROYAN

We are confronted with insurmountable opportunities.   POGO

Opportunities are usually disguised as hard work, so most people don't recognize them.   ANN LANDERS

When I look back now over my life and call to mind what I might have had simply for taking and did not take, my heart is like to break.   WILLIAM HALE WHITE

There is no security on this earth; there is only opportunity.

DOUGLAS MAC ARTHUR

Seize the opportunity by the beard, for it is bald behind.

BULGARIAN PROVERB

For the highest task of intelligence is to grasp and recognize genuine opportunity, possibility.   JOHN DEWEY

Half the pleasure of life consists of the opportunities one has neglected.   OLIVER WENDELL HOLMES, JR.

He who refuses to embrace a unique opportunity loses the prize as surely as if he tried and failed.   WILLIAM JAMES

One can present people with their opportunities. One cannot make them equal to them.   ROSAMOND LEHMANN

OPTIMISM

In these times you have to be an optimist to open your eyes when you awake in the morning. CARL SANDBURG

We have survived everything, and we have only survived it on our optimism. EDWARD STEICHEN

To the question whether I am a pessimist or an optimist, I answer that my knowledge is pessimistic, but my willing and hoping are optimistic. ALBERT SCHWEITZER

When people are happy, optimists are out of a job. AGNES REPPLIER

An optimist is a person who starts a crossword puzzle with a fountain pen. ANONYMOUS

An optimist is merely an ex-pessimist with his pockets full of money, his digestion in good condition, and his wife in the country. HELEN ROWLAND

Optimists do not wait for improvement; they achieve it. PAUL VON KEPPLER

A pessimist is a man who thinks all women are bad. An optimist is a man who hopes they are. CHAUNCEY DEPEW

I am an optimist. It does not seem too much use being anything else. SIR WINSTON CHURCHILL

ORATORY

Great oratory needs not merely the orator, but a great theme and a great occasion. LORD SAMUEL

The nature of oratory is such that there has always been a tendency among politicians and clergymen to oversimplify complex matters. From a pulpit or a platform even the most conscientious of speakers finds it very difficult to tell the whole truth. ALDOUS HUXLEY

In oratory the greatest art is to hide art. JONATHAN SWIFT

A man never becomes an orator if he has anything to say. FINLEY PETER DUNNE

Great oratory is great art, at its best to be reckoned among man's glories. But, not without reason, oratory has been called the harlot of the arts, so subject it is to abuse and degradation.

NORMAN THOMAS

Voice and manner were perhaps too much in the foreground of a speaker's thoughts in the old days of elocution and flowing oratory. I suspect that we have gone too far in neglect of them.

NORMAN THOMAS

Nothing is so unbelievable that oratory cannot make it acceptable.

CICERO

ORIGINALITY

The real originals now are the people who behave properly.

EDITH SITWELL

Originality is . . . a by-product of sincerity.   MARIANNE MOORE

Originality is simply a pair of fresh eyes.

THOMAS WENTWORTH HIGGINSON

The least of man's original emanation is better than the best of a borrowed thought.   ALBERT PINKHAM RYDER

Originality consists in depriving oneself of certain things. Personality asserts itself by its limitations.   ANDRÉ GIDE

Originality never expresses itself in harsh and obtrusive singularities.   COVENTRY PATMORE

The mark of highest originality lies in the ability to develop a familiar idea so fruitfully that it would seem no one else would ever have discovered so much to be hidden in it.   GOETHE

PARENTS

There may be some doubt as to who are the best people to have charge of children, but there can be no doubt that parents are the worst.   GEORGE BERNARD SHAW

The secret cruelties that parents visit upon their children are past belief.   DR. KARL A. MENNINGER

Parents may be fairly criticized for anything, with one exception— their children's behavior.   BRENDAN FRANCIS

Parenthood: That state of being better chaperoned than you were before marriage.   MARCELENE COX

To be a parent is almost to be a fatalist.

OLIVER WENDELL HOLMES, JR.

PARTY

No man does right by a woman at a party.   HARRY GOLDEN

Cocktail party: A gathering held to enable forty people to talk about themselves at the same time. The man who remains after the liquor is gone is the host.   FRED ALLEN

Whoever takes just plain ginger ale soon gets drowned out of the conversation.   KIN HUBBARD

When we are merriest, it is best to leave and drive home.

CZECH PROVERB

Even though the hour is late, it takes more determination than I've got to walk away from a party that is going well.

WILLIAM C. FEATHER

PAST

If you want to understand today, you have to search yesterday.

PEARL BUCK

Historic continuity with the past is not a duty, it is only a necessity.   OLIVER WENDELL HOLMES, JR.

It's never safe to be nostalgic about something until you're absolutely certain there's no chance of its coming back.   BILL VAUGHN

The past is not a package one can lay away.   EMILY DICKINSON

People move forward into the future out of the way they comprehend the past. When we don't understand something in our past, we are therefore crippled.   NORMAN MAILER

A man cannot free himself from the past more easily than he can from his own body.   ANDRÉ MAUROIS

When we think of the past we forget the fools and remember the sages. We reverse the process for our own time.   GEORGE BOAS

PATIENCE

Patience is a most necessary qualification for business; many a man would rather you heard his story than granted his request.

LORD CHESTERFIELD

Only those who have the patience to do simple things perfectly will acquire the skill to do difficult things easily.   JOHANN VON SCHILLER

Lack of pep is often mistaken for patience.   KIN HUBBARD

What is destructive is impatience, haste, expecting too much too fast.   MAY SARTON

Patience: A minor form of despair disguised as a virtue.

AMBROSE BIERCE

Patience is needed with everyone, but first of all with ourselves.

SAINT FRANCIS DE SALES

PEACE

Back of tranquillity lies always conquered unhappiness.

DAVID GRAYSON

Peace is when time doesn't matter as it passes by.   MARIA SCHELL

Almost all of us long for peace and freedom; but very few of us have much enthusiasm for the thoughts, feelings, and actions that make for peace and freedom.   ALDOUS HUXLEY

Great tranquility of heart is his who cares for neither praise nor blame.   THOMAS À KEMPIS

It takes two to make peace.   JOHN F. KENNEDY

PERSONALITY

The search for a new personality is futile; what is fruitful is the human interest the old personality can take in new activities.

CESARE PAVESE

The highest fortune of earth's children is always in their personality.   GOETHE

To confront with your personality all the other personalities of the earth.   WALT WHITMAN

Each needs to develop the sides of his personality which he has neglected.   ALEXIS CARREL

I think it is not well for any of us to allow another personality to submerge in any way our own.   OLIVE SCHREINER

PHOTOGRAPHY

No photographer is as good as the simplest camera.
EDWARD STEICHEN

The rarest thing in the world is a woman who is pleased with photographs of herself.   ELIZABETH METCALF

Pictures are wasted unless the motive power which impelled you to action is strong and stirring.   BERENICE ABBOTT

A great photograph is a full expression of what one feels about what is being photographed in the deepest sense, and is, thereby, a true expression of what one feels about life in its entirety.
ANSEL ADAMS

PLACE

I like to see a man proud of the place in which he lives. I like to see a man live so that his place will be proud of him. ABRAHAM LINCOLN

There is something always melancholy in the idea of leaving a place for the last time. It is like burying a friend.   ABIGAIL ADAMS

You can fall in love at first sight with a place as with a person.
ALEC WAUGH

Some places speak distinctly. Certain dank gardens cry aloud for a murder; certain old houses demand to be haunted; certain coasts are set apart for shipwrecks.   ROBERT LOUIS STEVENSON

How hard it is to escape from places. However carefully one goes they hold you—you leave little bits of yourself fluttering on the fences—little rags and shreds of your very life.
KATHERINE MANSFIELD

PLEASURE

And now the innocent pleasures of life. One must admit they have but one fault, they are so innocent.   SØREN KIERKEGAARD

A sense of wrongdoing is an enhancement of pleasure.
OLIVER WENDELL HOLMES, JR.

Illusion is the first of all pleasures.   VOLTAIRE

Whenever you are sincerely pleased, you are nourished.
RALPH WALDO EMERSON

There is something self-defeating in the too-conscious pursuit of pleasure.   MAX EASTMAN

I take it as a prime cause of the present confusion of society that it is too sickly and too doubtful to use pleasure frankly as a test of value.   REBECCA WEST

Get pleasure out of life . . . as much as you can. No one ever died from pleasure.   SOL HUROK

POETS AND POETRY

A poem is never finished, only abandoned.   PAUL VALÉRY

It is a sad fact about our culture that a poet can earn much more money writing or talking about his art than he can by practicing it.
W. H. AUDEN

Poetry? I too dislike it; there are things that are important beyond all this fiddle.   MARIANNE MOORE

The true poet is all the time a visionary and whether with friends or not, as much alone as a man on his death bed.   W. B. YEATS

Poets are mysterious, but a poet when all is said is not much more mysterious than a banker.   ALLEN TATE

A poet can survive everything but a misprint.   OSCAR WILDE

There never was a poet yet who could bear to have his wife say exactly what she thought of his poetry, any more than he would keep his temper if his wife beat him at chess.

CHARLES DUDLEY WARNER

I've had it with those cheap sons of bitches who claim they love poetry but never buy a book.   KENNETH REXROTH

The beautiful feeling after writing a poem is on the whole better even than after sex, and that's saying a lot.   ANNE SEXTON

Poetry is the language in which man explores his own amazement.
CHRISTOPHER FRY

Poetry is not a civilizer, rather the reverse, for great poetry appeals to the most primitive instincts. . . . It is a beautiful work of nature, like an eagle or a high sunrise.   ROBINSON JEFFERS

A copy of verses kept in the cabinet, and only shown to a few friends, is like a virgin much sought after and admired; but when printed and published, is like a common whore, whom anybody may purchase for half-a-crown.   JONATHAN SWIFT

POLITICS AND POLITICIANS

The hardest thing about any political campaign is how to win without proving that you are unworthy of winning.
ADLAI E. STEVENSON

Politicians neither love nor hate. Interest, not sentiment, directs them.   LORD CHESTERFIELD

Since a politician never believes what he says, he is surprised when others believe him.   CHARLES DE GAULLE

Politicians are the same all over. They promise to build a bridge even where there is no river.   NIKITA KHRUSHCHEV

A politician need never apologize for opportunism in action, but he should always be ashamed of compromise in thought.
WALTER BAGEHOT

The best thing about this group of candidates is that only one of them can win.   WILL ROGERS

Before you can begin to think about politics at all, you have to abandon the notion that here is a war between good men and bad men.   WALTER LIPPMANN

If you're in politics and you can't tell when you walk into a room who's for you and who's against you then you're in the wrong line of work.   LYNDON B. JOHNSON

We'd all like to vote for the best man, but he's never a candidate.   KIN HUBBARD

A political convention is just not a place where you come away with any trace of faith in human nature.   MURRAY KEMPTON

PORNOGRAPHY

A sodomite got very excited looking at a zoology text. Does this make it pornography?   STANISLAW J. LEC

If the purpose of pornography is to excite sexual desire, it is unnecessary for the young, inconvenient for the middle-aged, and unseemly for the old.   MALCOLM MUGGERIDGE

Pornography is supposed to arouse sexual desires. If pornography is a crime, when will they arrest makers of perfume?   RICHARD FLEISCHER

The facts are that pornography does not produce crime. Lack of it may.   DR. MARY S. CALDERONE

It'll be a sad day for sexual liberation when the pornography addict has to settle for the real thing.   BRENDAN FRANCIS

One inalienable right binds all mankind together—the right of self-abuse. That—and not the abuse of others—is what distinguishes the true lover of pornography. We would encourage him to seek his literary pleasure as and where he finds it.   KENNETH TYNAN

POSSESSIONS

Before we set our hearts too much on anything, let us examine how happy are those who already possess it.   LA ROCHEFOUCAULD

A man can hope for satisfaction and fulfillment only in what he does not yet possess; he cannot find pleasure in something of which he already has too much.   CARL G. JUNG

Everything you have wants to own you.   REGINA EILERT

The possession of a great many things, even the best of things, tends to blind one to the real value of anything. HOLBROOK JACKSON

The higher we ascend among human types and the more intense personalities become, the more the importance of possessions dwindles.   VIDA D. SCUDDER

Keep a thing seven years and it's bound to come in handy.

RUSSIAN PROVERB

POVERTY

Almsgiving tends to perpetuate poverty; aid does away with it once and for all.   EVA PERÓN

Every man has a right to be poor.   RICHARD JEFFERIES

Our affluent society contains those of talent and insight who are driven to prefer poverty, to choose it, rather than submit to the desolation of an empty abundance.   MICHAEL HARRINGTON

Only the poet has any right to be sorry for the poor, if he has anything to spare when he has thought of the dull, commonplace rich.   WILLIAM BOLITHO

Many a defect is seen in the poor man.   IRISH PROVERB

One of the strangest things about life is that the poor, who need money the most, are the very ones who never have it.

FINLEY PETER DUNNE

I'd like to live like a poor man with lots of money.   PABLO PICASSO

The only thing that can console one for being poor is extravagance.

OSCAR WILDE

The prevalent fear of poverty among the educated classes is the worst moral disease from which our civilization suffers.

WILLIAM JAMES

Poor people are not poor because they're dumb or because they're lazy but because society has not provided opportunity.

ANDREW YOUNG

POWER

The great secret of power is never to will to do more than you can accomplish.   HENRIK IBSEN

The imbecility of men is always inviting the impudence of power.

RALPH WALDO EMERSON

The qualities that get a man into power are not those that lead him, once established, to use power wisely.   LYMAN BRYSON

The only prize much cared for by the powerful is power. The prize of the general is not a bigger tent, but command.

OLIVER WENDELL HOLMES, JR.

Better to have a handful of might than a sack of justice.

CZECH PROVERB

PRAISE

Among the smaller duties of life I hardly know any one more important than that of not praising where praise is not due.

SYDNEY SMITH

You will only offend men by praise which suggests the limits of their worth.   VAUVENARGUES

Always when I see a man fond of praise I think it is because he is an affectionate man craving for affection.   W. B. YEATS

I have always said that if I were a rich man I would employ a professional praiser.   SIR OSBERT SITWELL

It is great to get praise from the lips of taciturnity.

JOHN ADDINGTON SYMONDS

Praises for our past triumphs are as feathers to a dead bird.

PAUL ELDRIDGE

If you call a thing bad you do little, if you call a thing good you do much.   GOETHE

PRAYER

In the life of the Indian there was only one inevitable duty—the duty of prayer—the daily recognition of the Unseen and Eternal.

OHIYESA,
of the Santee Dakotas

The trouble with our praying is, we just do it as a means of last resort.   WILL ROGERS

Prayer does not change God, but changes him who prays.

SØREN KIERKEGAARD

Complaint is the largest tribute heaven receives and the sincerest part of our devotion.   JONATHAN SWIFT

Might never prays.   BULGARIAN PROVERB

It is not well for a man to pray cream and live skim milk.

HENRY WARD BEECHER

He who prays for his neighbors will be heard for himself.

THE TALMUD

What I dislike the least in my former self are the moments of prayer.   ANDRÉ GIDE

PREACHING

If there is no hell, a good many preachers are obtaining money under false pretences.   WILLIAM A. ("BILLY") SUNDAY

It is a good divine that follows his own instructions.   SHAKESPEARE

The test of a preacher is that his congregation goes away saying, not "What a lovely sermon," but "I will do something about it."

SAINT FRANCIS DE SALES

Among provocatives, the next best thing to good preaching is bad preaching. I have even more thoughts during or enduring it than at other times.   RALPH WALDO EMERSON

The born preacher we feel instinctively to be our foe. He may do some good to the wretches who have been struck down and lie gasping on the battlefield: He rouses antagonism in the strong.

GEORGE MEREDITH

Preaching cannot be fruitful unless it is under the influence of the most tender compassion.   SAINT VINCENT FERRER

PREJUDICE

Bagels and lox for breakfast, soul food for lunch, and lasagna for dinner are great—but no Jews, blacks, or Italians on the professional or neighborhood turf!   ALICE ROSSI

It is never too late to give up our prejudices. HENRY DAVID THOREAU

For those who do not think, it is best at least to rearrange their prejudices once in a while.   LUTHER BURBANK

Our prejudices are like physical infirmities—we cannot do what they prevent us from doing.   JOHN LANCASTER SPALDING

Prejudices subsist in people's imagination long after they have been destroyed by their experience.   ERNEST DIMNET

Prejudice is never easy unless it can pass itself off for reason.
                                    WILLIAM HAZLITT

It is nowhere easier to break through all so-called prejudices than in the relations between a man and a woman.   HENRIK IBSEN

In overcoming prejudice, working together is even more effective than talking together.   RALPH W. SOCKMAN

PRESENT

There is something about the present which we would not exchange, though we were offered a choice of all past ages to live in.
                                    VIRGINIA WOOLF

Our faith in the present dies out long before our faith in the future.
                                    RUTH BENEDICT

The other day a man asked me what I thought was the best time of life. "Why," I answered without a thought, "now." DAVID GRAYSON

I don't think we understand the importance of the present; there's nothing more important than what you are doing now.
                                    HAROLD CLURMAN

Be in that which is still around you and which enters with an immeasurable past into the present that is yours.
                                    RAINER MARIA RILKE

PRESIDENCY

To please everybody is impossible; were I to undertake it, I should probably please nobody.   GEORGE WASHINGTON

The presidential office is not a rosewater affair. This is an office in which a man must put on his war paint.   WOODROW WILSON

The first twelve years are the hardest.   FRANKLIN D. ROOSEVELT

If you can sing a song that would make people forget their troubles and the Depression, I'll give you a medal.   HERBERT HOOVER,
to Rudy Vallee

Presidents in the past have always been better than their adversaries have predicted.   RUTHERFORD B. HAYES

They are the only friends I have who never pester me with their advice.   ANDREW JACKSON,
on some ten-year-olds

When the president fumbles, the whole goal line is wide open.
DEAN ACHESON

Presidents quickly realize that while a single act might destroy the world they live in, no one single decision can make life suddenly better or can turn history around for good.   LYNDON B. JOHNSON

He is . . . a kind of magnificent lion who can roam widely and do great deeds so long as he does not try to break loose from his broad reservation.   CLINTON ROSSITER

People want to be taken care of; they place ultimate responsibility for that on the president.   JAMES DAVID BARBER

If I hadn't been president of the United States, I probably would have ended up a piano player in a bawdy house. HARRY S. TRUMAN

There isn't any doubt but what a woman would make a good president.   HARRY S. TRUMAN

PRINCIPLE

Principles always become a matter of vehement discussion when practice is at an ebb.   GEORGE GISSING

When you say that you agree with a thing in principle you mean that you have not the slightest intention of carrying it out in practice.   OTTO VON BISMARCK

It is easier to fight for one's principles than to live up to them.

ALFRED ADLER

Many a man is acting on utilitarian principles, who is shocked at them in set treatises and disowns them.

JOHN HENRY CARDINAL NEWMAN

PROBLEM

Problems are the price you pay for progress.   BRANCH RICKEY

I had an immense advantage over many others dealing with the problem inasmuch as I had no fixed ideas derived from long-established practice to control and bias my mind, and did not suffer from the general belief that whatever is, is right. HENRY BESSEMER,
discoverer of a new method of producing steel

A great man is one who seizes the vital issue in a complex question, what we might call the "jugular vein" of the whole organism—and spends his energies upon that.   JOSEPH RICKABY

The best way to escape from a problem is to solve it.

BRENDAN FRANCIS

The most pleasant and useful persons are those who leave some of the problems of the universe for God to worry about. DON MARQUIS

Every solution of a problem is a new problem.   GOETHE

What a pity human beings can't exchange problems. Everyone knows exactly how to solve the other fellow's.   OLIN MILLER

PROCRASTINATION

Procrastination is the art of keeping up with yesterday.

DON MARQUIS

In putting off what one has to do, one runs the risk of never being able to do it.   CHARLES BAUDELAIRE

Tomorrow is often the busiest day of the week.   SPANISH PROVERB

Nothing is so fatiguing as the eternal hanging on of an uncompleted task.   WILLIAM JAMES

PROSTITUTION

Prostitutes, more than any other profession, help keep American marriages together.   BRENDAN FRANCIS

A perfect whore should, like the fabled Proteus of old, be able to assume every form, and to vary the attitudes of pleasure according to the times, circumstances, and temperaments.

"THE WHORE'S CATECHISM"

I like prostitution. My heart has never failed to pound at the sight of one of those provocatively dressed women walking in the rain under the gas lamps, just as the sight of monks in their robes and knotted girdles touches some ascetic, hidden corner of my soul.

GUSTAVE FLAUBERT

If you spit in a harlot's eye, she says it's raining.   YIDDISH PROVERB

I never once went to a prostitute, maybe because so many enthusiastic amateurs were around.   A. S. NEILL

I've only hated men at those moments when I realized that I was doing all the giving and they the taking. At least when I was a prostitute, it was all honest and up-front.   XAVIERA HOLLANDER

> She was "honeychile," in New Orleans,
> The hottest of the bunch;
> But on the old expense account,
> She was gas, cigars, and lunch.

ANONYMOUS

PUBLISHER

Publishers are demons, there's no doubt about it.   WILLIAM JAMES

Another illusion, seldom entertained by competent authors, is that the publisher's readers and others are waiting to plagiarize their work. I think it may be said that the more worthless the manuscript, the greater the fear of plagiarism.   SIR STANLEY UNWIN

Great editors do not discover or produce great authors; great authors create and produce great publishers.   JOHN FARRAR

Publishing is a very mysterious business. It is hard to predict what kind of sale or reception a book will have, and advertising seems to do very little good.   THOMAS WOLFE

No publisher should ever express an opinion of the values of what he publishes. That is a matter entirely for the literary critic to decide.   OSCAR WILDE

PURPOSE

Great minds have purposes, others have wishes. WASHINGTON IRVING

Continuity of purpose is one of the most essential ingredients of happiness in the long run, and for most men this comes chiefly through their work.   BERTRAND RUSSELL

Without some goal and some effort to reach it, no man can live.
                                                FYODOR DOSTOEVSKI

To have no set purpose in one's life is the harlotry of the will.
                                                STEPHEN MAC KENNA

QUARREL

Most quarrels are inevitable at the time; incredible afterwards.
                                                E. M. FORSTER

In real life it takes only one to make a quarrel.   OGDEN NASH

For souls in growth, great quarrels are great emancipators.
                                                LOGAN PEARSALL SMITH

A quarrel that is unavoidable . . . is likely to be less bitter if the battlers hold off long enough to take a bite of food.
                                                ARTHUR T. JERSILD

Quarreling binds men as closely as other things.   CHARLES PÉGUY

An association of men who will not quarrel with one another is a thing which never yet existed, from the greatest confederacy of nations down to a town meeting or a vestry.   THOMAS JEFFERSON

QUESTION

Better ask ten times than go astray once.   YIDDISH PROVERB

A good question is never answered. It is not a bolt to be tightened
into place but a seed to be planted and to bear more seed toward
the hope of greening the landscape of idea.   JOHN CIARDI

If we would have new knowledge, we must get a whole world of
new questions.   SUSAN K. LANGER

It is better to stir up a question without deciding it, than to decide
it without stirring it up.   JOSEPH JOUBERT

To be able to ask a question clearly is two-thirds of the way to
getting it answered.   JOHN RUSKIN

QUOTATION

I often quote myself; it adds spice to my conversation.
                                    GEORGE BERNARD SHAW

The art of quotation requires more delicacy in the practice than
those conceive who can see nothing more in a quotation than an
extract.   BENJAMIN DISRAELI

Every quotation contributes something to the stability or enlarge-
ment of the language.   SAMUEL JOHNSON

He wrapped himself in quotations—as a beggar would enfold himself in the purple of emperors.   RUDYARD KIPLING

I will not say that he willfully misquotes, but he does fail to quote
accurately.   ABRAHAM LINCOLN

The power of quotation is as dreadful a weapon as any which the
human intellect can forge.   JOHN JAY CHAPMAN

Have you ever observed that we pay much more attention to a
wise passage when it is quoted, than when we read it in the original author?   PHILIP G. HAMERTON

To be amused by what you read—that is the great spring of happy
quotations.   C. E. MONTAGUE

The profoundest thought or passion sleeps as in a mine, until an
equal mind and heart finds and publishes it.
                                    RALPH WALDO EMERSON

It is the little writer rather than the great writer who seems never
to quote, and the reason is that he is never really doing anything
else.   HAVELOCK ELLIS

READING

We can never know that a piece of writing is bad unless we have begun by trying to read it as if it was very good and ended by discovering that we were paying the author an undeserved compliment.   C. S. LEWIS

Those who reproach an author for being obscure should first look inside themselves to see how much light there is in them. GOETHE

The school system has much to say these days of the virtue of reading widely, and not enough about the virtues of reading less but in depth.   JOHN CIARDI

There are times when I think that the reading I have done in the past has had no effect except to cloud my mind and make me indecisive.   ROBERTSON DAVIES

One gets more fun out of the novels that are not great than out of the great ones.   OLIVER WENDELL HOLMES, JR.

As readers, we remain in the nursery stage so long as we cannot distinguish between taste and judgment, so long, that is, as the only possible verdicts we can pass on a book are two: this I like; this I don't like.   W. H. AUDEN

I read forever and am determined to sacrifice my eyes like John Milton rather than give up the amusement without which I should despair.   JOHN ADAMS

Nothing is worth reading that does not require an alert mind.
                                                      CHARLES DUDLEY WARNER

I move my lips when I read—I'm painfully slow—so I like really good English.   JOHN LE CARRE

We read to say that we have read.   CHARLES LAMB

To acquire the habit of reading is to construct for yourself a refuge from almost all the miseries of life.   W. SOMERSET MAUGHAM

REALITY

It is and it must in the long run be better for man to see things as they are than to be ignorant of them.   A. E. HOUSEMAN

The stupendous fact that we stand in the midst of reality will always be something far more wonderful than anything else we do.

ERICH GUTKIND

How hard it is, sometimes, to trust the evidence of one's senses! How reluctantly the mind consents to reality! NORMAN DOUGLAS

Some people are still unaware that reality contains unparalleled beauties. The fantastic and unexpected, the ever-changing and renewing is nowhere so exemplified as in real life itself.

BERENICE ABBOTT

A man might pass for insane who should see things as they are.

WILLIAM ELLERY CHANNING

Set up as an ideal the facing of reality as honestly and as cheerfully as possible. DR. KARL A. MENNINGER

Somehow, if you really attend to the real, it tells you everything.

ROBERT C. POLLOCK

When you see yourself in proportion—as you're bound to do when you get some sense—then you see how much greater what is real is than anything you can put down. EUDORA WELTY

REASON

Truly, that reason upon which we plume ourselves, though it may answer for little things, yet for great decisions is hardly surer than a toss-up. CHARLES SANDERS PEIRCE

If you follow reason far enough it always leads to conclusions that are contrary to reason. SAMUEL BUTLER

The vast majority of human beings are not interested in reason or satisfied with what it teaches. Nor is reason itself the most satisfactory instrument for the understanding of life. ALDOUS HUXLEY

Reason means truth and those who are not governed by it take the chance that someday the sunken fact will rip the bottom out of their boat. OLIVER WENDELL HOLMES, JR.

All men have a reason, but not all men can give a reason.

JOHN HENRY CARDINAL NEWMAN

If we would be guided by the light of reason, we must let our minds be bold. LOUIS BRANDEIS

I'll not listen to reason. Reason always means what someone else
has got to say.   ELIZABETH GASKELL

REFORM AND REFORMERS

Reform often seems only the dislike of the blasé for the people with
animal spirits.   FRANK MOORE COLBY

I mean to cut off all my dissolute acquaintance, leave off wine and
carnal company, and betake myself to politics and decorum.
                                                  LORD BYRON

Every reform, however necessary, will by weak minds be carried to
an excess which will itself need reforming.
                                      SAMUEL TAYLOR COLERIDGE

The trouble is that everyone talks about reforming others, and no
one thinks about reforming himself.   SAINT PETER OF ALCANTARA

Reformers, as a group, are not a very attractive group of people. As
you get older you recognize that. They are too self-righteous. They
feel that they have the call.   ROBERT MOSES

All reformers, however strict their social conscience, live in houses
just as big as they can pay for.   LOGAN PEARSALL SMITH

Like all other zealous reformers, we do what we do because we like
doing it better than anything else.   DON MARQUIS

RELIGION

Whatever you are be a good one.   ABRAHAM LINCOLN

It is usually when men are at their most religious that they behave
with the least sense and the greatest cruelty.   ILKA CHASE

Don't stay away from church because there are so many hypo-
crites. There's always room for one more.   A. R. ADAMS

True religion is a matter for belief and not for controversies. It is a
matter of experience and not of historical or philosophical demon-
strations.   REMY DE GOURMONT

We have just enough religion to make us hate, but not enough to
make us love one another.   JONATHAN SWIFT

A man who should act, for one day, on the supposition that all the people about him were influenced by the religion which they professed would find himself ruined by night.   THOMAS MACAULAY

A religion can no more afford to degrade its Devil than to degrade its God.   HAVELOCK ELLIS

No rage is equal to the rage of a contented right-thinking man when he is confronted in the marketplace by an idea which belongs in the pulpit.   THURMAN W. ARNOLD

I was just thinking, if it is really religion with these nudist colonies, they sure must turn atheists in the wintertime.   WILL ROGERS

What a travesty to think religion means saving my little soul through my little good deeds and the rest of the world go hang.

GERALD VANN

REPUTATION

The only time you realize you have a reputation is when you're not living up to it.   JOSÉ ITURBI

It is difficult to make a reputation, but it is even more difficult to mar a reputation once properly made—so faithful is the public.

ARNOLD BENNETT

Reputation is in itself only a farthing candle, of a wavering and uncertain flame, and easily blown out, but it is the light by which the world looks for and finds merit.   JAMES RUSSELL LOWELL

RESPONSIBILITY

The buck stops with the guy who signs the checks.

RUPERT MURDOCH

It seems to me that any full grown, mature adult would have a desire to be responsible, to help where he can in a world that needs so very much, that threatens us so very much.   NORMAN LEAR

A new position of responsibility will usually show a man to be a far stronger creature than was supposed.   WILLIAM JAMES

Few things help an individual more than to place responsibility upon him, and to let him know that you trust him.

BOOKER T. WASHINGTON

The great thought, the great concern, the great anxiety of men is to restrict, as much as possible, the limits of their own responsibility.

GIOSUÉ BORSI

REST

To work is simple enough; but to rest, there is the difficulty.

ERNEST HELLO

A day out-of-doors, someone I loved to talk with, a good book and some simple food and music—that would be rest.

ELEANOR ROOSEVELT

We should rest and amuse ourselves in such a way that rest and amusement do not become an additional fatigue or a total waste of time.   ALEXIS CARREL

A good rest is half the work.   YUGOSLAV PROVERB

Take rest; a field that has rested gives a bountiful crop.   OVID

RETIREMENT

Retiring must not mean just vegetating. I don't think anybody can do that.   EDWARD STEICHEN

Sooner or later I'm going to die, but I'm not going to retire.

MARGARET MEAD

Don't simply retire *from* something; have something to retire *to*.

HARRY EMERSON FOSDICK

I felt after reaching ninety-two it was time to sleep in the morning if I chose to do so, and I have a lot of projects of my own to work on.   JUDGE HAROLD R. MEDINA

A retired husband is often a wife's full-time job.   ELLA HARRIS

RIGHT

It's an odd thing about this universe that, though we all disagree with each other, we are all of us always in the right.

LOGAN PEARSALL SMITH

Even when we know what is right, too often we fail to act. More often we grab greedily for the day, letting tomorrow bring what it will, putting off the unpleasant and unpopular.

BERNARD M. BARUCH

If you want things to be right you have to do them yourself.

JACQUELINE ONASSIS

We are not satisfied to be right, unless we can prove others to be quite wrong.   WILLIAM HAZLITT

Human beings are perhaps never more frightening than when they are convinced beyond doubt that they are right.

LAURENS VAN DER POST

RIGHTS

If some people got their rights they would complain of being deprived of their wrongs.   OLIVER HERFORD

Silence never won rights. They are not handed down from above; they are forced by pressures from below.   ROGER BALDWIN

Human rights are the natural outgrowth of people becoming culturally and economically secure. As you become secure, you want to be freer.   ANDREW YOUNG

Be as beneficent as the sun or the sea, but if your rights as a rational being are trenched on, die on the first inch of your territory.   RALPH WALDO EMERSON

No man was ever endowed with a right without being at the same time saddled with a responsibility.   GERALD W. JOHNSON

It is in the concrete, and not in the abstract, that rights prevail in every sound and wholesome society.   FRANCIS PARKMAN

RUSSIA AND THE RUSSIANS

Russia is a country that no matter what you say about it, it's true. Even if it's a lie, it's true.   WILL ROGERS

Russia is a country that buries its troubles. Your criticism is your epitaph. You simply say your say and then you're through.

WILL ROGERS

The Russians' objectives have not altered, despite the hot winds and the cold which blow from the Kremlin.   BERNARD M. BARUCH

Russians are very isolated from cultural differences. They're terribly uncomfortable and insecure around blacks, and every African knows it.   ANDREW YOUNG

Everybody has always underrated the Russians. They keep their own secrets alike from foe and friends.   SIR WINSTON CHURCHILL

They love to keep you waiting . . . but they hate you to deviate from a plan you once make!   ELEANOR ROOSEVELT

SEA

Most of us, I suppose, are a little nervous of the sea. No matter what its smiles may be, we doubt its friendship.   H. M. TOMLINSON

We all like to see people seasick when we are not ourselves.   MARK TWAIN

Why do we love the sea? It is because it has some potent power to make us think things we like to think.   ROBERT HENRI

There is indeed, perhaps, no better way to hold communion with the sea than sitting in the sun on the veranda of a fishermen's cafe.   JOSEPH W. BEACH

The true peace of God begins at any spot a thousand miles from the nearest land.   JOSEPH CONRAD

The great sea makes one a great sceptic.   RICHARD JEFFERIES

SELF

A man who finds no satisfaction in himself, seeks for it in vain elsewhere.   LA ROCHEFOUCAULD

It is a great mistake to fancy oneself greater than one is, and to value oneself at less than one is worth.   GOETHE

There is hardly one in three of us who live in the cities who is not sick with unused self.   BEN HECHT

To conquer oneself is a greater task than conquering others.   BUDDHA

"Be yourself" is about the worst advice you can give some people.

TOM MASSON

What we have to be is what we are.   THOMAS MERTON

Trying to define yourself is like trying to bite your own teeth.

ALAN WATTS

What a man thinks of himself, that it is which determines, or rather indicates his fate.   HENRY DAVID THOREAU

If I despised myself, it would be no compensation if everyone saluted me, and if I respect myself, it does not trouble me if others hold me lightly.   MAX NORDAU

I am much better employed from every point of view, when I live solely for my own satisfaction, than when I begin to worry about the world. The world frightens me, and a frightened man is no good for anything.   GEORGE GISSING

One finds one's way only by taking it.   A. D. SERTILLANGES

No one remains quite what he was when he recognizes himself.

THOMAS MANN

Nothing said to us, nothing we can learn from others, reaches us so deep as that which we find in ourselves.   THEODORE REIK

SEX

Clock strikes—going out to make love. Somewhat perilous but not disagreeable.   LORD BYRON

We're still a sexophobic society, afraid of the wrong things for the wrong reasons.   DR. MARY S. CALDERONE

Do we really want our fourteen- and fifteen-year-olds to believe the message we beam to them continually—that you're not with it until you've had it?   DR. MARY S. CALDERONE

When I was young, I used to have successes with women because I was young. Now I have successes with women because I am old. Middle age was the hardest part.   ARTHUR RUBINSTEIN

When you have found the place where a woman loves to be fondled, don't you be ashamed to touch it any more than she is.

OVID

As for promiscuous kissing, what decent girl wants to resemble a piece of rock salt licked by all kinds and conditions of passing cattle?   S. PARKES CADMAN

What matters is not the length of the wand, but the magic in the stick.   ANONYMOUS

Sex should be put in its proper place. It should be extolled and deified.   BERNARD MAC FADDEN

One patient swore to his doctor that his performance was greatly enhanced by eating a sausage pizza. This must be considered a unique experience!   DR. RICHARD MILSTEN

The main problem with honest women is not how to seduce them, · but how to take them to a private place. Their virtue hinges on half-open doors.   JEAN GIRAUDOUX

The tragedy of sexual intercourse is the perpetual virginity of the soul.   WILLIAM B. YEATS

Whoever called it necking was a poor judge of anatomy.

GROUCHO MARX

A mistress should be like a little country retreat near the town; not to dwell in constantly but only for a night and away.

WILLIAM WYCHERLY

I think the people who like sex stay home. I mean I don't think they make a big thing out of it.   NELSON ALGREN

I *don't* like being a sex object. I find that unappealing and I understand why women don't like it—because it's not good for your ego. You're replaceable.   DUSTIN HOFFMAN

Sex is the only mysticism offered by materialism, whose other toys—like motor-cars and airplanes and moving pictures and swimming pools and flights to the moon—soon pall.

MALCOLM MUGGERIDGE

I am not promiscuous, you know. Promiscuity implies that attraction is not necessary.   TALLULAH BANKHEAD

Today the emphasis is on sex, and very little on the beauty of sexual relationship. Contemporary books and films portray it like a contest, which is absurd.   HENRY MILLER

SILENCE

It is good speaking that improves good silence.   DUTCH PROVERB

The silent bear no witness against themselves.   ALDOUS HUXLEY

Silence alone is great; all else is weakness.   ALFRED DE VIGNY

He who does not understand your silence will probably not understand your words.   ELBERT HUBBARD

One man may teach another to speak, but none can teach another to hold his peace.   POLISH PROVERB

The greatest events—are not our noisiest, but our stillest hours.
FRIEDRICH NIETZSCHE

Accustomed to the veneer of noise, to the shibboleths of promotion, public relations, and market research, society is suspicious of those who value silence.   JOHN LAHR

SINCERITY

I should say sincerity, a deep, great, genuine sincerity, is the characteristic of all men in any way heroic.   THOMAS CARLYLE

A little sincerity is a dangerous thing, and a great deal of it is absolutely fatal.   OSCAR WILDE

The most exhausting thing in life is being insincere.
ANNE MORROW LINDBERGH

It is possible by long-continued practice, not merely in lying, but in talking on subjects in which we have no real interest, not to know when we are sincere and when we are not.   MARK RUTHERFORD

A word from the heart goes straight to the heart.   ABBÉ HUVELIN

I know not from what nonsense world the notion first came: that there is some connection between being sincere and being semi-articulate.   G. K. CHESTERTON

I don't think you want too much sincerity in society. It would be like an iron girder in a house of cards.   W. SOMERSET MAUGHAM

SLEEP

Early to rise and early to bed makes a male healthy and wealthy and dead.   JAMES THURBER

The sun has not caught me in bed in fifty years. THOMAS JEFFERSON

Insomnia is a gross feeder. It will nourish itself on any kind of thinking, including thinking about not thinking. CLIFTON FADIMAN

The day will happen whether or not you get up.   JOHN CIARDI

Luxury is an ancient notion. There was once a Chinese mandarin who had himself wakened three times every morning simply for the pleasure of being told it was not yet time to get up.   ARGOSY

Sleep faster, we need the pillows.   YIDDISH PROVERB

No human being believes that any other human being has a right to be in bed when he himself is up.   ROBERT LYND

SMOKING

Now, I've given up cigarettes, for me there is no such thing as smoking in moderation.   CARL SANDBURG

I never smoked a cigarette until I was nine.   W. C. FIELDS

Smoke your pipe and be silent; there's only wind and smoke in the world.   IRISH PROVERB

I am disturbed when I see a cigarette between the lips or fingers of some important person upon whose intelligence and judgment the welfare of the world in part depends.   LINUS PAULING

There's something luxurious about having a girl light your cigarette. In fact, I got married once on account of that.

HAROLD ROBBINS

It has always been my rule never to smoke when asleep, and never to refrain when awake.   MARK TWAIN

To be sure, it is a shocking thing, blowing smoke out of our mouths into other people's mouths, eyes, and noses, and having the same thing done to us.   SAMUEL JOHNSON

Thank heaven, I have given up smoking again! . . . God! I feel fit. Homicidal, but fit. A different man. Irritable, moody, depressed, rude, nervy, perhaps; but the lungs are fine.   A. P. HERBERT

SOCIETY

Society is always engaged in a vast conspiracy to preserve itself—at the expense of the new demands of each new generation.

JOHN HAYNES HOLMES

Society is, in general, profoundly indifferent and forgetful.

ANDRÉ MAUROIS

Man becomes free, not by realizing himself in opposition to society, but by realizing himself through society.

CHRISTOPHER CAULDWELL

I think societal instinct much deeper than sex instinct—and societal repression much more devasting.   D. H. LAWRENCE

Despite all efforts, things are badly ordered for the soul in human society.   ALFRED ADLER

SOLITUDE

No man should go through life without once experiencing healthy, even bored solitude in the wilderness, finding himself depending solely on himself and thereby learning his true and hidden strength.   JACK KEROUAC

The happiest of all lives is a busy solitude.   VOLTAIRE

We live in a very tense society. We are pulled apart . . . and we all need to learn how to pull ourselves together. . . . I think that at least part of the answer lies in solitude.   HELEN HAYES

The great omission in American life is solitude; not loneliness, for this is an alienation that thrives most in the midst of crowds, but that zone of time and space, free from the outside pressures, which is the incubator of the spirit.   MARYA MANNES

It is this horror of solitude, this need to lose his *ego* in exterior flesh, which man calls grandly *the need for love*.   CHARLES BAUDELAIRE

The solitude which is really injurious is the severance from all who are capable of understanding us.   PHILIP G. HAMERTON

SORROW

Grief is a species of idleness.   SAMUEL JOHNSON

No matter how one's heart aches, one can do the necessary things and do them well.   MYRTLE REED

Where there is sorrow, there is holy ground.   OSCAR WILDE

Sorrow is like a precious treasure, shown only to friends.
                                        AFRICAN PROVERB

Sorrow you can hold, however desolating, if nobody speaks to you. If they speak, you break down.   BEDE JARRETT

This, like our other ups and downs, is but for a little while in world history, but the moment has its right to sorrow, however much one may look beyond.   OLIVER WENDELL HOLMES, JR.

Tears dry,
Don't ask me why.

                                        CANDY JONES

Sorrow makes us all children again—destroys all differences of intellect. The wisest know nothing.   RALPH WALDO EMERSON

No one can keep his griefs in their prime; they use themselves up.
                                        E. M. CIORAN

All sorrows can be borne if you put them into a story or tell a story about them.   ISAK DINESEN

SPEECH

If you're offered an *honorarium* for a speech, you can be sure the money is of no *consequencium*.   MERLE MILLER

It usually takes me more than three weeks to prepare a good impromptu speech.   MARK TWAIN

Why doesn't the fellow who says, "I'm no speechmaker," let it go at that instead of giving a demonstration?   KIN HUBBARD

Be sincere; be brief; be seated.   FRANKLIN D. ROOSEVELT,
                                            advice to his son James
                                            on speechmaking

I sometimes marvel at the extraordinary docility with which Americans submit to speeches.   ADLAI E. STEVENSON

A good speech is a good thing, but the verdict is the thing.
                                            DANIEL O'CONNELL

Prolonged statistics are a lethal dose, which if it does not kill will certainly dispel your audience.   ILKA CHASE

I would lay emphasis above all things, on the speaking voice. People rely far too much on that deceptive gadget, the microphone.
                                            CORNELIA OTIS SKINNER

My basic rule is to speak slowly and simply so that my audience has an opportunity to follow and think about what I am saying.
                                            MARGARET CHASE SMITH

A speech should be made as though you are taking off a pair of long white gloves, which can only be done very slowly. . . . You ease into your talk so that by the time you get to what you came to say, your audience is with you.   LIZ CARPENTER,
                                            quoting a speech teacher

One must not only believe in what one is saying but also that it matters, especially that it matters to the people to whom one is speaking.   NORMAN THOMAS

Always be shorter than anybody dared to hope.   LORD READING

There's plenty of great advice available about the art of making talks, but if you don't adapt it to yourself, none of it is worth much.   JUDY LANGFORD CARTER

SUCCESS

It's the hardest thing in the world to accept a *little* success and leave it that way.   MARLON BRANDO

There is only one success—to be able to spend your life in your own way.   CHRISTOPHER MORLEY

To find a career to which you are adapted by nature, and then to work hard at it, is about as near to a formula for success and happiness as the world provides.   MARK SULLIVAN

Success to me is having ten honeydew melons and eating only the top half of each one.   BARBRA STREISAND

The penalty of success is to be bored by the people who used to snub you.   LADY ASTOR

The great secret of success is to go through life as a man who never gets used up.   ALBERT SCHWEITZER

The fastest way to succeed is to look as if you're playing by other people's rules, while quietly playing by your own.   MICHAEL KORDA

I was successful because you believed in me.   ULYSSES S. GRANT,
to Abraham Lincoln

Victory won't come to me unless I go to it.   MARIANNE MOORE

What is success? It is a toy balloon among children armed with pins.   GENE FOWLER

To follow, without halt, one aim: There's the secret of success.
ANNA PAVLOVA

There is nothing in the world that will take the chip off of one's shoulder like a feeling of success.   THOMAS WOLFE

Success is not always a sure sign of merit, but it is a first-rate way to succeed.   JOSH BILLINGS

For one man who sincerely pities our misfortunes, there are a thousand who sincerely hate our success.   CHARLES CALEB COLTON

SUFFERING

He who fears he will suffer, already suffers because of his fear.
MONTAIGNE

Think occasionally of the suffering of which you spare yourself the sight.   ALBERT SCHWEITZER

To have become a deeper man is the privilege of those who have suffered.   OSCAR WILDE

The best way to dim one's pain is to cast it in the shadow of one's sympathy.   JOHN ANDREW HOLMES

TALENT

If a man has a talent and learns somehow to use the whole of it, he has gloriously succeeded, and won a satisfaction and a triumph that few men ever know.   THOMAS WOLFE

It is a very rare thing for a man of talent to succeed by his talent.
                                                        JOSEPH ROUX

A genuine talent finds its way.   GOETHE

Genius and stupidity never stray from their respective paths; talent wanders to and fro, following every light.   GEORGE MOORE

There is no such thing as talent. There is pressure.   ALFRED ADLER

One can never really explain a man or track talent to its lair; and all attempts to do so are works of the imagination.
                                                 JOHN JAY CHAPMAN

Everyone has talent; what is rare is the courage to follow the talent to the dark place where it leads.   ERICA JONG

TASTE

The kind of people who always go on about whether a thing is in good taste invariably have very bad taste.   JOE ORTON

Good taste is the worst vice ever invented.   EDITH SITWELL

Our tastes often improve at the expense of our happiness.
                                                     JULES RENARD

A private railroad car is not an acquired taste. One takes to it immediately.   MRS. AUGUST BELMONT

In every power, of which taste is the foundation, excellence is pretty fairly divided between the sexes.   JANE AUSTEN

More women use their eyes for pleasure than do men, and this has been true in America for a long time. In our country, decisions of visual taste traditionally have been left to women.   RUSSELL LYNES

The only real elegance is in the mind; if you've got that, the rest really comes from it.   DIANA VREELAND

TAXES

Income tax has made more liars out of the American people than golf has.   WILL ROGERS

To tax and to please, no more than to love and to be wise, is not given to men.   EDMUND BURKE

Today, it takes more brains and effort to make out the income-tax form than it does to make the income.   ALFRED E. NEUMAN

The hardest thing in the world to understand is the income tax.
                                                    ALBERT EINSTEIN

Of all debts, men are least willing to pay their taxes; what a satire this is on government.   RALPH WALDO EMERSON

Lying is not taxed.   SPANISH PROVERB

If the Lord loveth a cheerful giver, how he must hate the taxpayer!
                                                   JOHN ANDREW HOLMES

What is the difference between a taxidermist and a tax collector? The taxidermist takes only your skin.   MARK TWAIN

TEACHING

Everything I learn about teaching I learn from bad students.
                                                          JOHN HOLT

Of all the excellent teachers of college English whom I have known I have never discovered one who knew precisely what he was doing. Therein have lain their power and their charm.
                                                   MARY ELLEN CHASE

When all is said and done, the fact remains that some teachers have a naturally inspiring presence, and can make their exercises interesting, while others simply cannot.   WILLIAM JAMES

There are just a few things a teacher can do, and that only for the sensitive and the spirited.   IRWIN EDMAN

No man, however conservative, can stand before a class day after day and refrain from saying more than he knows.   MORRIS COHEN

Do not blame teachers or their administrators if they fail to educate, to change their students. For the task of *preventing* the new generation from changing in any deep or significant way is precisely what most societies require of their educators.

GEORGE B. LEONARD

Teaching school is but another name for sure and not very slow destruction.   THOMAS CARLYLE

People sometimes say, "I should like to teach if only pupils cared to learn." But then there would be little need of teaching.

GEORGE HERBERT PALMER

Students rarely disappoint teachers who assure them in advance that they are doomed to failure.   SIDNEY HOOK

TELEPHONE

I'd rather sit down and write a letter than call someone up. I hate the telephone.   HENRY MILLER

In heaven when the blessed use the telephone they will say what they have to say and not a word besides.   W. SOMERSET MAUGHAM

Middle age: When you're sitting at home on Saturday night and the telephone rings and you hope it isn't for you.   OGDEN NASH

A woman is a person who reaches for a chair when she answers the telephone.   MILTON WRIGHT

When a telephone rings, the average man settles deeper into his chair with the observation, "I wonder who that can be?"

MARCELENE COX

TELEVISION

Watching Dinah Shore for just one week is like being imprisoned inside a giant butterscotch sundae.   HARRY F. WATERS,
TV editor of Newsweek

Television was not intended to make human beings vacuous, but it is an emanation of their vacuity.   MALCOLM MUGGERIDGE

Everything is for the eye these days—TV, *Life, Look,* the movies. Nothing is just for the mind. The next generation will have eyeballs as big as cantaloupes and no brain at all.   FRED ALLEN

Radio was a tragedy for the deaf. Television is a tragedy for the blind. It is also, on occasion, a tragedy for the sensitive viewer to whom the contemplation of mediocrity is a painful experience.

STEVE ALLEN

One man's mediocrity is another man's good program.

DR. FRANK STANTON

Television is now so desperately hungry for material that they're scraping the top of the barrel.   GORE VIDAL

What compels you [Americans] to stare, night after night, at all the glittering hokum that has been deliberately put together for you?   J. B. PRIESTLEY

There are days when any electrical appliance in the house, including the vacuum cleaner, seems to offer more entertainment possibilities than the TV set.   HARRIET VAN HORNE

TENNIS

All top players are the same strokewise, but mentally I can improve and that's where it's at for top players.

MARTINA NAVRATILOVA

Tennis is an addiction that once it has truly hooked a man will not let him go.   RUSSELL LYNES

Don't compose eulogies to yourself when you get ahead. Concentrate on staying there.   ROD LAVER

A champion is afraid of losing; everyone else is afraid of winning.

BILLIE JEAN KING

Tennis belongs to the individualistic past—a hero, or at most a pair of friends or lovers, against the world.   JACQUES BARZUN

Tennis does not often reward creativity. The man who can master the prosaic may be unexciting, but he is usually successful.

EUGENE SCOTT

In no game played with a ball is concentration a greater virtue than in tennis.   ALLISON DANZIG

THOUGHT

Thinking is like loving and dying. Each of us must do it for himself.   JOSIAH ROYCE

Thought is the universal consoler.   NICHOLAS DE CHAMFORT

The number of substitutes for fine and clean thinking the world
provides positively gnaws at one's vitals.   HAROLD J. LASKI

If we were all to be judged by our thoughts, the hills would be
swarming with outlaws.   JOHANN SIGURJONSSON

I like to think of thoughts as living blossoms borne by the human
tree.   JAMES DOUGLAS

It is well for people who think, to change their minds occasionally
in order to keep them clean.   LUTHER BURBANK

The best we can do for one another is to exchange our thoughts
freely; and that, after all, is about all.   JAMES FROUDE

Thought is so rare an essence that wherever we discover a man-
ifestation of it we not only relish it but are tempted to approve of
it.   HENRI DE LUBAC

No amount of energy will take the place of thought. A strenuous
life with its eyes shut is a kind of wild insanity.   HENRY VAN DYKE

What, oh what, oh what is thought? It is the only thing—and yet
nothing.   JOHN ADDINGTON SYMONDS

It is stupidity to suppress what comes into one's mind.
                                          HINDU PROVERB

Thought is great and swift and free, the light of the world, and the
chief glory of man.   BERTRAND RUSSELL

The free man is he who does not fear to go to the end of his
thought.   LÉON BLUM

TIME

Who forces time is pushed back by time; who yields to time finds
time on his side.   THE TALMUD

The more a person is able to direct his life consciously, the more he can use time for constructive benefits.   ROLLO MAY

Time: All things consume it, love alone makes use of it.

PAUL CLAUDEL

What can be done at any time is never done at all.

ENGLISH PROVERB

If you want work well done, select a busy man—the other kind has no time.   ELBERT HUBBARD

It has been left to our generation to discover that you can move heaven and earth to save five minutes and then not have the faintest idea what to do with them when you have saved them.

C. E. M. JOAD

It was a book to kill time for those who like it better dead.

ROSE MACAULAY

Ordinary people merely think how they shall *spend* their time; a man of talent tries to *use* it.   ARTHUR SCHOPENHAUER

TRAVEL

I traveled a good deal all over the world, and I got along pretty good in all these foreign countries, for I have a theory that it's their country and they got a right to run it like they want to.

WILL ROGERS

Too often travel, instead of broadening the mind, merely lengthens the conversation.   ELIZABETH DREW

Now, in the space of a few hours we can travel from one continent to another. . . . It's killed all the joy of travel. It would be wonderful to set out on a donkey, like Stevenson. That's the way to see a country.   HENRY MILLER

The best things in travel are all undesigned, and perhaps even undeserved.   H. M. TOMLINSON

A man travels the world over in search of what he needs and returns home to find it.   GEORGE MOORE

I dislike feeling at home when I am abroad. GEORGE BERNARD SHAW

I soon realized that no journey carries one far unless, as it extends into the world around us, it goes an equal distance into the world within.   LILLIAN SMITH

I think that travel comes from some deep urge to see the world, like the urge that brings up a worm in an Irish bog to see the moon when it is full.   LORD DUNSANY

TROUBLE

There are people who are always anticipating trouble, and in this way they manage to enjoy many sorrows that never really happen to them.   JOSH BILLINGS

If you want to make someone laugh, tell him your troubles, Maria.
                                                        SPANISH PROVERB

When one has too great a dread of what is impending, one feels some relief when the trouble has come.   JOSEPH JOUBERT

Most of the trouble in the world is caused by people wanting to be important.   T. S. ELIOT

He who will live for others shall have great troubles, but they shall seem to him small. He who will live for himself shall have small troubles, but they shall seem to him great.   WILLIAM R. INGE

Bygone troubles are good to tell.   YIDDISH PROVERB

When in trouble one remembers Allah.   AFRICAN PROVERB

The usual excuse of those who cause others trouble is that they wish them well.   VAUVENARGUES

There is nothing so consoling as to find that one's neighbor's troubles are at least as great as one's own.   GEORGE MOORE

TRUST

Our distrust is very expensive.   RALPH WALDO EMERSON

One must be fond of people and trust them if one is not to make a mess of life.   E. M. FORSTER

I think we may safely trust a good deal more than we do.

HENRY DAVID THOREAU

You may be deceived if you trust too much, but you will live in torment unless you trust enough.   DR. FRANK CRANE

TRUTH

The truth brings with it a great measure of absolution, always.

R. D. LAING

Truth is always exciting. Speak it, then. Life is dull without it.

PEARL BUCK

Men ardently pursue truth, assuming it will be angels' bread when found.   W. MACNEILE DIXON

Like all valuable commodities, truth is often counterfeited.

JAMES CARDINAL GIBBONS

When one has one's hand full of truth it is not always wise to open it.   FRENCH PROVERB

When I tell any truth, it is not for the sake of convincing those who do not know it, but for the sake of defending those that do.

WILLIAM BLAKE

It is one of the maladies of our age to profess a frenzied allegiance to truth in unimportant matters, to refuse consistently to face her where graver issues are at stake.   NORMAN DOUGLAS

A curse on every wish that blurs the sight, paralyzes the tongue, cramps the hand, and prevents the truth being seen, said, and written.   THEODOR HAECKER

The truth is the only thing worth having, and, in a civilized life, like ours, where so many risks are removed, facing it is almost the only courageous thing left to do.   E. V. LUCAS

I tore myself away from the safe comfort of certainties through my love for truth; and truth rewarded me.   SIMONE DE BEAUVOIR

UNDERSTANDING

Light comes to us unexpectedly and obliquely. Perhaps it amuses the gods to try us. They want to see whether we are asleep.

H. M. TOMLINSON

It is difficult to get a man to understand something when his salary depends upon his not understanding it.   UPTON SINCLAIR

I have suffered from being misunderstood, but I would have suffered a hell of a lot more if I had been understood.

CLARENCE DARROW

Brevity is very good when we are, or are not, understood.

SAMUEL BUTLER

Understanding a person does not mean condoning; it only means that one does not accuse him as if one were God or a judge placed above him.   ERICH FROMM

Understanding is the beginning of approving. To negate with conviction one must never have looked at what one negates.

ANDRÉ GIDE

To understand any living thing, you must, so to say, creep within and feel the beating of its heart.   W. MACNEILE DIXON

People who do not understand themselves have a craving for understanding.   DR. WILHELM STEKEL

UNIQUENESS

How glorious it is—and also how painful—to be an exception.

ALFRED DE MUSSET

It is in part the very uniqueness of every individual that makes him, not only a member of a family, race, nation, or class, but a human being.   HELEN MERRELL LYND

Even in ordinary social intercourse the most delicate compliment is to treat the person with whom you are talking as an exception to all rules.   SAMUEL MC CHORD CROTHERS

Every man is more than just himself; he also represents the unique, the very special and always significant and remarkable point at which the world's phenomena intersect, only once in this way and never again.   HERMANN HESSE

In order to be irreplaceable one must always be different.

COCO CHANEL

There lurks, perhaps, in every human heart a desire of distinction, which inclines every man first to hope, and then to believe, that Nature has given him something peculiar to himself.

SAMUEL JOHNSON

UNIVERSE

Maybe creating itself is all the fun the universe gets. DON MARQUIS

Be an opener of doors for such as come after thee, and do not try to make the universe a blind alley. RALPH WALDO EMERSON

The conflict of forces and the struggle of opposing wills are of the essence of our universe and alone hold it together. HAVELOCK ELLIS

The complete man is man with the universe. ROBERT C. POLLOCK

Not unfortunately the universe is wild—game-flavoured as a hawk's wing. B. P. BLOOD

VACATION

No man needs a vacation so much as the person who has just had one. ELBERT HUBBARD

A vacation is what you take when you can no longer take what you've been taking. EARL WILSON

The choice and nature of our holidays is more perhaps than anything in our lives an expression of ourselves. ALEC WAUGH

Girls who are having a good sex thing stay in New York. The rest want to spend their summer vacations in Europe. GAIL PARENT

It has long been my belief that in times of great stress, such as a four-day vacation, the thin veneer of family unity wears off almost at once, and we are revealed in our true personalities.

SHIRLEY JACKSON

A good vacation is over when you begin to yearn for your work.

DR. MORRIS FISHBEIN

Nearly everybody underestimates the price of a vacation.

WILLIAM C. FEATHER

A vacation frequently means that the family goes away for a rest, accompanied by mother, who sees that the others get it.

MARCELENE COX

Holidays are enticing only for the first week or so. After that, it is no longer such a novelty to rise late and have little to do.

MARGARET LAURENCE

Merely changing the scenery doesn't make for much of a holiday, especially if one continues to do the same things. GEORGE SANDERS

VANITY

You'd better not go about injuring people's vanity—it is the tenderest spot they have.   AUGUST STRINDBERG

She is a peacock in everything but beauty.   OSCAR WILDE

A man is ever apt to contemplate himself out of all proportion to his surroundings.   CHRISTINA G. ROSSETTI

O blessed conceit, what should we be without you?

RUDYARD KIPLING

Most of us retain enough of the theological attitude to think that we are little gods.   OLIVER WENDELL HOLMES, JR.

A vain man can never be utterly ruthless: He wants to win applause and therefore he accommodates himself to others. GOETHE

Most of us would be far enough from vanity if we heard all the things that are said about us.   JOSEPH RICKABY

To this principle of vanity, which philosophers call a mean one, and which I do not, I owe a great part of the figure which I have made in life.   LORD CHESTERFIELD

He was like a cock who thought the sun had risen to hear him crow.   GEORGE ELIOT

VICE

The vices of the rich and great are mistaken for error; and those of the poor and lowly, for crimes.   LADY MARGUERITE BLESSINGTON

I don't say we all ought to misbehave, but we ought to look as if we could.   ORSON WELLES

Vice is perhaps the desire to know everything. HONORÉ DE BALZAC

There is more than a morsel of truth in the saying, "He who hates vice hates mankind."   W. MAC NEILE DIXON

It has ever been my experience that folks who have no vices, have very few virtues.   ABRAHAM LINCOLN

Never support two weaknesses at the same time. It's your combination sinners—your lecherous liars and your miserly drunkards—who dishonor the vices and bring them into bad repute.

THORNTON WILDER

Loud indignation against vice often stands for virtue in the eyes of bigots.   J. PETIT-SENN

Ingenuity is required even for the practice of vice. HINDU PROVERB

VIOLENCE

There is a great streak of violence in every human being. If it is not channeled and understood, it will break out in war or in madness.

SAM PECKINPAH

Nine-tenths of mankind are more afraid of violence than of anything else; and inconsistent moderation is always popular, because of all qualities it is the most opposite to violence. WALTER BAGEHOT

I'm terribly violent. I've often had the urge to kill. I love knives, blades, not revolvers—they make an absurd noise—no, a silent blade with a fine taper.   COLETTE

Violence commands both literature and life, and violence is always crude and distorted.   ELLEN GLASGOW

Violence attempts to constrain the other's freedom, to force him to act in the way we desire, but with ultimate lack of concern, with indifference to the other's own existence or destiny.   R. D. LAING

We are all shot through with enough motives to make a massacre, any day of the week that we want to give them their head.

JACOB BRONOWSKI

VIRTUE

Virtues are as dangerous as vices insofar as they are allowed to rule over one as authorities and not as qualities one develops oneself.

FRIEDRICH NIETZSCHE

Nothing is more unpleasant than a virtuous person with a mean mind.   WALTER BAGEHOT

Woman's virtue is man's greatest invention. CORNELIA OTIS SKINNER

We are more inclined to regret our virtues than our vices; but only the very honest will admit this.   HOLBROOK JACKSON

It is a revenge the devil sometimes takes upon the virtuous, that he entraps them by the force of the very passion they have suppressed and think themselves superior to.   GEORGE SANTAYANA

The highest virtue here may be least in another world.

KAHLIL GIBRAN

Beware of making your moral staple consist of the negative virtues.

OLIVER WENDELL HOLMES, JR.

We are double-edged blades, and every time we whet our virtue the return stroke strops our vice.   HENRY DAVID THOREAU

Virtue has always been conceived of as victorious resistance to one's vital desire to do this, that, or the other.

JAMES BRANCH CABELL

VOICE

Shut me up in a dark room with a multitude and I can pick out the gentlefolk by their voices.   THOMAS WENTWORTH HIGGINSON

I would rather be kicked with a foot than be overcome by a loud voice speaking cruel words.   ELIZABETH BARRETT BROWNING

People have to talk about something just to keep their voice boxes in working order, so they'll have good voice boxes in case there's ever anything really meaningful to say.   KURT VONNEGUT, JR.

A good voice can transform the most conventional of sermons into something like a divine revelation.   ALDOUS HUXLEY

To expect to rule others by assuming a loud tone is like thinking oneself tall by putting on high heels.   J. PETIT-SENN

Men will always delight in a woman whose voice is lined with velvet.   BRENDAN FRANCIS

WAITING

To him that waits all things reveal themselves, provided that he has the courage not to deny, in the darkness, what he has seen in the light.   COVENTRY PATMORE

Punctuality on the part of a woman we desire is not a pleasure commensurable with the pain she causes us when she is late.

PAUL-JEAN TOULET

The future belongs to him who knows how to wait.

RUSSIAN PROVERB

We do not obtain the most precious gifts by going in search of them but by waiting for them.   SIMONE WEIL

We may assume that we keep people waiting symbolically because we do not wish to see them and that our anxiety is due not to being late, but to our having to see them at all.   CYRIL CONNOLLY

People count up the faults of those who keep them waiting.

FRENCH PROVERB

All comes at the proper time to him who knows how to wait.

SAINT VINCENT DE PAUL

WALKING

Walking isn't a lost art—one must, by some means, get to the garage.   EVAN ESAR

Thoughts come clearly while one walks.   THOMAS MANN

I represent what is left of a vanishing race, and that is the pedestrian. . . . That I am still able to be here, I owe to a keen eye and a nimble pair of legs. But I know they'll get me someday.

WILL ROGERS

To enjoy walking merely as walking was—and is—considered an eccentricity in the United States.   EDNA FERBER

I like long walks, especially when they're taken by people who annoy me.   FRED ALLEN

WAR

No country is so wild and difficult but men will make it a theater
of war.   AMBROSE BIERCE

The first casualty when war comes is truth.   HIRAM JOHNSON

If you want to know when a war might be coming, you just watch
the U.S. and see when it starts cutting down on its defenses. It's the
surest barometer in the world.   WILL ROGERS

Those who do not go to war roar like lions.   KURDISH PROVERB

We have failed to grasp the fact that mankind is becoming a single
unit, and that for a unit to fight against itself is suicide.
                                                      HAVELOCK ELLIS

What is absurd and monstrous about war is that men who have no
personal quarrel should be trained to murder one another in cold
blood.   ALDOUS HUXLEY

I love war and responsibility and excitement. Peace is going to be
hell on me.   GEORGE S. PATTON

War is sweet to those who have not experienced it.   ERASMUS

Our modern wars make many unhappy while they last and none
happy when they are over.   GOETHE

Fundamentally, public opinion wins wars.   DWIGHT D. EISENHOWER

War has a deeper and more ineffable relation to hidden grandeurs
in man than has yet been deciphered.   THOMAS DE QUINCEY

There is hardly such a thing as a war in which it makes no difference who wins. Nearly always one side stands more or less for
progress, the other side more or less for reaction.   GEORGE ORWELL

When you are winning a war almost everything that happens can
be claimed to be right and wise.   SIR WINSTON CHURCHILL

WIFE

Never make a toil of pleasure, as Billy Ban said when he dug his
wife's grave only three feet deep.   SEUMAS MAC MANUS

I think ten mistresses are better than one wife. Since I'm a good husband, I can only dream.   ISAAC ASIMOV

Among Majorcan peasants who live beyond the tourist range, no man would ever think of buying or selling so much as a hen without his wife's approval.   ROBERT GRAVES

No laborer in the world is expected to work for room, board, and love—except the housewife.   LETTY COTTIN POGREBIN

What man could stand a perfect wife?   JUVENAL

I submit to my fellow dramatists that the unfaithfulness of a wife is no longer a subject for drama, but only for comedy.

W. SOMERSET MAUGHAM

Young wives are the leading asset of corporate power. They want the suburbs, a house, a settled life, and respectability. They want society to see that they have exchanged themselves for something of value.   RALPH NADER

The reason they're called the opposite sex is because every time you think you have your wife fooled—it's just the opposite!

WALTER WINCHELL

To avoid mistakes and regrets, always consult your wife before engaging in a flirtation.   E. W. HOWE

If our wives don't treat us as they should, we ought to be very grateful.   ANONYMOUS

By all means marry; if you get a good wife, you'll become happy; if you get a bad one, you'll become a philosopher.   SOCRATES

No man expects a great deal from marriage. He is quite satisfied if his wife is a good cook, a good valet, an attentive audience, and a patient nurse.   ANONYMOUS

I have learned that only two things are necessary to keep one's wife happy. First let her think she's having her way. And second let her have it.   LYNDON B. JOHNSON

He took misfortune like a man—blamed it on his wife.

BRIGID DE VINE

I've been reading a lot lately about Indian captives. One woman who had been captured by the Indians and made a squaw was resentful when she was rescued because she'd found that there was a lot more work to do as the wife of a white man.

STEPHEN VINCENT BENÉT

What is instinct? It is the natural tendency in one when filled with dismay to turn to his wife.   FINLEY PETER DUNNE

If you want peace in the house, do what your wife wants.

AFRICAN PROVERB

No man prospers without the consent and cooperation of his wife.

ABIGAIL ADAMS

My wife tells me she doesn't care what I do when I'm away, as long as I'm not enjoying it.   LEE TREVINO,
on touring

My affection for a certain lady (you know who, my dear) quickens my affection for everybody else that does not deserve my hatred.

JOHN ADAMS

WINNING

To win you have to risk loss.   JEAN-CLAUDE KILLY

Nobody remembers who came in second.   CHARLES SCHULZ

Winning is living. Every time you win, you're reborn. When you lose, you die a little.   GEORGE ALLEN

When you win, nothing hurts.   JOE NAMATH

Nothing can seem foul to those that win.   SHAKESPEARE

Winning isn't everything, but it beats anything that comes in second.   PAUL W. ("BEAR") BRYANT

I'd rather be a poor winner than any kind of loser.

GEORGE S. KAUFMAN

I win because winning is right on, it's honest. Your blood turns sour and sticky when you lose.   JOE KAPP

WISDOM

Wisdom before experience is only words; wisdom after experience is of no avail.   MARK VAN DOREN

Wisdom consists not so much in knowing what to do in the ultimate as knowing what to do next.   HERBERT HOOVER

I believe that all wisdom consists in caring immensely for a few right things, and not caring a straw about the rest.   JOHN BUCHAN

The art of being wise is the art of knowing what to overlook.
WILLIAM JAMES

The wisdom of the wise is an uncommon degree of common sense.
WILLIAM R. INGE

The older I grow the more I distrust the familiar doctrine that age brings wisdom.   H. L. MENCKEN

Growth in wisdom may be exactly measured by decrease in bitterness.   FRIEDRICH NIETZSCHE

The attempt to combine wisdom and power has only rarely been successful and then only for a short while.   ALBERT EINSTEIN

WOMAN

A woman without a man is like a fish without a bicycle.
GLORIA STEINEM

Women have very little idea of how much men hate them.
GERMAINE GREER

Women are like elephants to me. I like to look at them, but I wouldn't want to own one.   W. C. FIELDS

Women are not inherently passive or peaceful. We're not inherently anything but human.   ROBIN MORGAN

A highbrow is a man who has found something more interesting than women.   EDGAR WALLACE

"No" is no negative in a woman's mouth.   SIR PHILIP SIDNEY

It has been well said that the position which women hold in a country is, if not a complete test, yet one of the best tests of the progress it has made in civilization.   JAMES BRYCE

When they try to assert themselves as the equals of men they become unendurable.   GEORGE SANDERS

No man is as antifeminist as a really feminine woman.

FRANK O'CONNOR

I can't be a rose in any man's lapel.   MARGARET TRUDEAU

Women are not the weak, frail little flowers that they are advertised. There has never been anything invented yet, including war, that a man would enter into, that a woman wouldn't, too.

WILL ROGERS

One woman's poise is another woman's poison.   KATHERINE BRUSH

The supply of good women far exceeds that of the men who deserve them.   ROBERT GRAVES

Contrary to general opinion, women are not so sentimental as men, but are much more hardheaded.   TAYLOR CALDWELL

The feminine mystique has succeeded in burying millions of American women alive.   BETTY FRIEDAN

The myth of the strong black woman is the other side of the coin of the myth of the beautiful dumb blonde.   ELDRIDGE CLEAVER

Women who make men talk better than they are accustomed to are always popular.   E. V. LUCAS

When I see the elaborate study and ingenuity displayed by women in the pursuit of trifles, I feel no doubt of their capacity for the most herculean undertakings.   JULIA WARD HOWE

To tell a woman everything she may not do is to tell her what she can do.   SPANISH PROVERB

I have an idea that the phrase "weaker sex" was coined by some woman to disarm some man she was preparing to overwhelm.

OGDEN NASH

Whatever women do they must do twice as well as men to be thought half as good. Luckily, this is not difficult.

CHARLOTTE WHITTON,
former mayor Ottawa, Canada

Nobody objects to a woman being a good writer or sculptor or geneticist if at the same time she manages to be a good wife, a good mother, good-looking, good-tempered, well-dressed, well-groomed, and unaggressive.   MARYA MANNES

American women are fools because they try to be everything to everybody.   VIVA

WORDS

Words are seductive and dangerous material to be used with caution.   BARBARA TUCHMAN

You can stroke people with words.   F. SCOTT FITZGERALD

Oh, words are action good enough, if they're the right words.
                                                    D. H. LAWRENCE

We are much at the mercy of words. They govern our thoughts more often than they obey them.   J. MIDDLETON MURRY

Broadly speaking, the short words are the best, and the old words best of all.   SIR WINSTON CHURCHILL

Unhappy is a people that has run out of words to describe what is going on.   THURMAN ARNOLD

It is astonishing what power words have over man.
                                                    NAPOLEON BONAPARTE

Better one word before than two after.   WELSH PROVERB

WORK

People who work sitting down get paid more than people who work standing up.   OGDEN NASH

Work is the only thing. Life may bring disappointments, but work is consolation.   MARCEL PROUST

The footprint of the owner is the best manure.   ENGLISH PROVERB

If a man love the labour of any trade apart from any question of success or fame, the gods have called him. ROBERT LOUIS STEVENSON

Anyone can do any amount of work, provided it isn't the work he is supposed to be doing at that moment.   ROBERT BENCHLEY

When I work I relax; doing nothing or entertaining visitors makes me tired.   PABLO PICASSO

Work isn't to make money; you work to justify life. MARC CHAGALL

More men are killed by overwork than the importance of this world justifies.   RUDYARD KIPLING

Everything considered, work is less boring than amusement.

CHARLES BAUDELAIRE

Without doubt half the ethical rules they din into our ears are designed to keep us at work.   LLEWELYN POWYS

I have come finally to a simple philosophy of work. I enjoy what I do and do the best I can. That is enough.   MARIA SCHELL

When love and skill work together, expect a masterpiece.

JOHN RUSKIN

My father taught me to work; he did not teach me to love it.

ABRAHAM LINCOLN

The better work men do is always done under stress and at great personal cost.   WILLIAM CARLOS WILLIAMS

All the best work is done the way the ants do things—by tiny but untiring and regular additions.   LAFCADIO HEARN

WORLD

I soon found out you can't change the world. The best you can do is to learn to live with it.   HENRY MILLER

There is no appeal from the ways of the world, which must continue on its own terms or take us all down with it into chaos and confusion.   MARK VAN DOREN

Men have never known what the world is moving to.

HAVELOCK ELLIS

The most incomprehensible thing about the world is that it is comprehensible.   ALBERT EINSTEIN

He who rebukes the world is rebuked by the world.

RUDYARD KIPLING

The most beautiful thing in the world is, of course, the world itself.

WALLACE STEVENS

This is still a world in which too many of the wrong things happen somewhere. But this is a world in which we now have the means to make a great many more of the right things happen everywhere.

MARGARET MEAD

The world is moving so fast these days that the man who says it can't be done is generally interrupted by someone doing it.

ELBERT HUBBARD

The reasonable man adapts himself to the world: The unreasonable one persists in trying to adapt the world to himself. Therefore all progress depends on the unreasonable man.

GEORGE BERNARD SHAW

WRITERS AND WRITING

Bad authors are those who write with reference to an inner context which the reader cannot know.   ALBERT CAMUS

If you let conditions stop you from working, they'll always stop you.   JAMES T. FARRELL

Nobody writes if they have had a happy childhood.

JOSEPH HERGESHEIMER

The secret of style is, after all, the mystery of the clothing of a flower.   ZONA GALE

I think that as you learn more about writing you learn to be direct.

EUDORA WELTY

Loafing is the most productive part of a writer's life.

JAMES NORMAN HALL

Only a mediocre writer is always at his best.

W. SOMERSET MAUGHAM

The only real gauge of success we have is profit—honest profit.

REX BEACH

I'm not happy when I'm writing, but I'm more unhappy when I'm not.   FANNIE HURST

There's no way anybody can sit down and write a best seller.

HAROLD ROBBINS

I make it a rule to sit at my desk eight hours a day whether anything's happening or not.   TED ("DR. SEUSS") GEISEL

The most difficult thing in the world is to make things simple enough, and enticing enough, to cause readers to turn the page.

HELEN GURLEY BROWN

It is impossible to discourage the real writers—they don't give a damn what you say, they're going to write.   SINCLAIR LEWIS

An author in his book must be like God in the universe, present everywhere and visible nowhere.   GUSTAVE FLAUBERT

All authentic writing comes from an individual; but a final judgment of it will depend not on how much individuality it contains, but how much of common humanity.   JOHN PEALE BISHOP

WRONG

Freedom is the right to be wrong, not the right to do wrong.

JOHN DIEFENBAKER

I may have faults but being wrong ain't one of them. JIMMY HOFFA

I don't like these cold, precise, perfect people, who, in order not to speak wrong, never speak at all, and in order not to do wrong, never do anything.   HENRY WARD BEECHER

As long as the world shall last there will be wrongs, and if no man objected and no man rebelled, those wrongs would last forever.

CLARENCE DARROW

Those who are fond of setting things to rights have no great objection to seeing them wrong.   WILLIAM HAZLITT

The worst-tempered people I've ever met were people who knew they were wrong.   WILSON MIZNER

YOUTH

I can't take seriously anyone who worries about the judgment of young people.   PAUL VALÉRY

To be young is to be held back.   ANDRÉ MALRAUX

Young people are surprisingly frail, in spite of their ebullient spirits and elasticity, and there are times when misfortune or unkindness will destroy them.   PATRICK O'BRIEN

American youth attributes much more importance to arriving at driver's-license age than at voting age.   MARSHALL MC LUHAN

Even the youngest among us is not infallible.   BENJAMIN JOWETT

Young men have a passion for regarding their elders as senile.

HENRY ADAMS

Fear of corrupting the mind of the younger generation is the loftiest form of cowardice.   HOLBROOK JACKSON

I never felt that there was anything enviable in youth. I cannot recall that any of us, as youths, admired our condition to excess or had a desire to prolong it.   BERNARD BERENSON

How different from the present was the youth of earlier days.

OVID, A.D. 15

Youth has to do with spirit, not age. Men of seventy and eighty are often more youthful than the young. Theirs is the real youth.

HENRY MILLER

A generation without a cause in its youth has no legacy in its old age.   EDWARD M. KENNEDY

It's a grand thing to see a young girl walking the road. J. M. SYNGE

INDEX OF AUTHORS

Time, 146
Tolstoy, Leo, 14, 30, 104, 130
Tomita, Kojiro, 16
Tomlinson, H. M., 172, 186, 188
Toulet, Paul-Jean, 130, 194
Toynbee, Arnold, 44
Tremayne, Sydney, 130
Trevino, Lee, 197
Trevor-Roper, H. R., 92
Trilling, Diana, 80
Trilling, Lionel, 27
Trotsky, Leon, 106
Trudeau, Margaret, 199
Trudeau, Pierre Elliot, 58
Truman, Bess, 84
Truman, Harry S., 78, 97, 161
Tuchman, Barbara, 200
Tugwell, Rexford Guy, 100
Tunney, Gene, 31, 124
Turner, Lana, 54
Twain, Mark, 2, 29, 35, 47, 55, 59, 76 77, 84, 87, 99, 114, 135, 147, 148, 172, 176, 178, 182
Tynan, Kenneth, 23, 156

Unamuno, Miguel de, 77, 134
Unitas, Johnny, 87
Unwin, Sir Stanley, 163

Valéry, Paul, 9, 136, 154, 203
Vanbrugh, Sir John, 4, 54
Van der Post, Laurens, 106, 171
Van Doren, Mark, 197, 201
Van Dyke, Henry, 51, 84, 185
Van Horne, Harriet, 51, 184
Vann, Gerald, 102, 169
Van Vechten, Carl, 36
Vaudable, Louis, 60
Vaughn, Bill, 151
Vauvenargues, 1, 35, 98, 104, 158, 186
Veeck, Bill, 19
Velimirovic, Nicholai, 48
Vidal, Gore, 12, 184
Vigny, Alfred de, 94, 175
Vincent de Paul, Saint, 51, 106, 118, 194
Vincent Ferrer, Saint, 159
Virgil, 76
Viva, 200
Voltaire, 29, 104, 154, 177
Von Keppler, Paul, 149
Vonnegut, Kurt, Jr., 193
Vreeland, Diana, 80, 137, 181

Walker, James J., 36, 121
Wallace, Edgar, 139, 198
Walters, Barbara, 115
Warhol, Andy, 23, 137

Warner, Charles Dudley, 49, 68, 83, 154, 166
Warner, Pop, 87
Warren, Earl, 103
Washington, Booker T., 169
Washington, George, 37, 160
Washington, Martha, 17
Waters, Harry F., 183
Watts, Alan, 28, 130, 173
Waugh, Alec, 153, 190
Waugh, Evelyn, 81
Weil, Simone, 22, 94, 194
Weininger, Otto, 73, 80
Welch, Raquel, 126
Welles, Orson, 191
Wells, H. G., 67, 89, 141
Wells, Joe E., 96
Welsh proverb, 47, 62, 121, 126, 200
Welty, Eudora, 167, 202
West, Jessamyn, 14, 34, 136
West, Mae, 27, 79
West, Rebecca, 16, 101, 136, 154
Wharton, Edith, 45, 115
Wheelock, John Hall, 66
Whistler, James McNeill, 17
White, E. B., 91, 145
White, William Allen, 8
White, William Hale, 3, 9, 23, 148
Whitehead, Alfred North, 4, 25, 44, 90, 94, 98, 114, 123, 141
Whitman, Walt, 35, 72, 88, 113, 147, 153
Whitton, Charlotte, 199
Whore's Catechism, The, 163
Wilde, Oscar, 4, 15, 16, 27, 39, 40, 47, 59, 65, 74, 78, 95, 109, 112, 116, 128, 154, 157, 164, 175, 178, 180, 191
Wilder, Thornton, 1, 4, 50, 143, 192
Williams, Msgr. Henry H., 41
Williams, Ted, 19
Williams, Tennessee, 25
Williams, William Carlos, 129, 201
Willour, Margaret, 8
Wilson, Earl, 18, 190
Wilson, Woodrow, 38, 135, 161
Winchell, Walter, 196
Windsor, Duke of, 11
Winters, Shelley, 105
Wintu Indian woman, An old, 66
Wittgenstein, Ludwig, 121
Wodehouse, P. G., 61
Wolfe, Thomas, 11, 116, 164, 180, 181
Wooden, John, 20
Woolf, Virginia, 135, 148, 160
Woollcott, Alexander, 8, 53, 122
Wright, Frank Lloyd, 138
Wright, Milton, 183
Wrigley, Philip K., 38, 139
Wrigley, William, Jr., 34
Wycherly, William, 174